Bathing-Machines and Bloomers

Muriel V. Searle

MIDAS BOOKS

Also in Midas' *Heritage of the Past* series
Victorians on the Thames by Reginald Bolland
Fairs and Revels by Brian Jewell
Port Out, Starboard Home by Anna Sproule
Sports and Games — history and origins by Brian Jewell
Spas and Watering-Places by Muriel Searle

Jacket: *Mermaids at Brighton* by Cruikshank, 1820
Endpapers: *Bathing-Machines at Brighton* by Thomas Rowlandson

First published 1977 by
MIDAS BOOKS
12 Dene Way, Speldhurst,
Tunbridge Wells, Kent TN3 0NX

© Muriel Searle 1977
Designed by Brian Jewell

ISBN 0 85936 089 X

Printed in Scotland
by John G Eccles Printers Ltd, Inverness.

Contents

Queen Victoria's
bathing-machine

1.   The Good of George the Third

George the First was always reckoned
Vile. But viler George the Second.
And what mortal ever heard
Any good of George the Third?

So runs an old favourite among school history-class ditties, originally penned with tongue in cheek by the rhyming Victorian wit Walter Savage Landor.

What *could* be found to say in favour of George III or any other king and his monotonously repeated dates of birth, accession and death, as foisted upon us of the great legion of history-haters by teachers, tomes and textbooks? How poorly they compared with the merits of more believable figures, such as fathers, mothers, aunts and engine-drivers who, when blessed Saturday came around, might be relied on to transport us away from that noble army of Georges, Williams and Edwards to the summer seaside.

Yet, little though we realised it, to the detested George III of our history books we owed the very notion of taking excursions and holidays by the sea for health and pleasure. Chiefly to his setting of a new fashion we owed the whole character of the English seaside town and its traditional pastimes, from the standardised layout of beach, promenade and residential terraces to the recognition of bathing and paddling as acceptable pastimes for anyone from a king to a coster-monger; from games on the sand to strolling before breakfast or after dinner along the 'prom-prom-prom-tiddly-om-pom-pom'. Windsor Castle and sandcastles had more in common than we imagined.

If we chanced to live in the West Country, our Saturdays might well have been spent where the national seaside cult as we now know it is generally said to have been born, paddling at the very spot where George III was first drawn in a creaking bathing-machine to plant a shivering royal toe into the salty surf, daringly sampling for himself at Weymouth the new-fangled business of sea bathing.

Until then, bathing had been followed only on a modest scale at various tiny and undeveloped spots around his kingdom's coast, fishing ports and hamlets whose growth into huge modern resorts spreading for miles, simply by virtue of the appeal of bathing and sunshine, must have appeared utterly absurd had any prophet foretold it.

Scarborough in about 1900, a typical English seaside resort of Georgian origin.

5

Four decades before George III arrived, Weymouth showed its first signs of beach life on the very humblest level, two local men being granted permission to erect a pair of primitive wooden bathing-sheds near the harbour that was then the town's sole prosperity. By 1768, according to the diary of a schoolboy visitor, a handful of bathing-machines had appeared, as yet such a novelty as to merit an entry: 'The bay is very fine, and as good a beach for bathing as any in England; convenient machines for that purpose are drawn into the sea by one horse.' Not until 1785 was an esplanade first mentioned in local records, but Weymouth still merited only the description 'a decayed seaport' rather than 'a rising resort.' That state was not to come upon it for another four years.

Scarcely since Elizabeth I's day had embryonic Weymouth witnessed such an array of well-shod horses, fine-crested carriages, ladies luxuriating in laces, dandies upholstered with velvet padded with banknotes and duchesses practising courtly artificial mannerliness, each attended by droves of maids and servants, as when George III clattered into the small port from Windsor, despatched thither with Queen Charlotte and a brace of princesses by his progressively-minded physicians, whose recommendation for convalescence following a serious illness was this new therapy of sea bathing, hitherto little followed by the gentry and only tentatively by a few commoners living near the coast. Bringing up the rear at a barely respectful distance came a motley platoon of a breed that was even then as old as time, a gaggle of celebrity-spotters drawn to the spectacle like human iron filings to a magnet. They were the advance guard of many, attracted from miles around, who would converge on suddenly-regalised Weymouth to stare, stare and stare

Weymouth Esplanade much as George III would have known it.

6

Weymouth, cradle of the bathing-machine, in about 1910, when bathing-machines were still a major source of income.

again at a monarch whose main desire was privacy, a commodity as far beyond the reach of a public figure as a crown was beyond a Dorset yokel or fisherman. It would not be long before these were joined by more pretentious name-droppers, better heeled but not necessarily better bred, clambering aboard the royal bandwagon on its subsequent visits because being seen in the right place at the right time by the right people automatically meant keeping up with the court.

Weymouth appeared uninspiring to this company of socialites uprooted from gay London and Windsor. Only sporadic development fringed its dreary new esplanade, and accommodation of style was, to say the least, at a premium. The only way in which a minor aristocrat or jumped-up rich man could house his family and servants within suitable proximity to the royal party was to build from scratch for himself. Thus, directly it became clear that King George had taken to the bathing-machine like the proverbial duck to water and obviously intended to return season after season, a wave of new buildings swept along the shoreline. Spacious houses and terraces appeared, in the elegantly-proportioned and classical geometrical style that was currently fashionable, those same terraces which still dominate Weymouth today and make it one of our best examples of a harmoniously-planned Georgian seaside resort.

The King himself adopted as a modest royal residence the Duke of Gloucester's old home of Gloucester Lodge, afterwards the Gloucester Hotel, where even the cabinet was obliged periodically to present itself for important business, making the place a mini-Westminster.

For a while, on his first, eleven-week, visit, the invalid King was not permitted actually to immerse himself in the water but was introduced gradually to its benefits through sea-water baths taken at Gloucester Lodge in a cumbersome hollowed-out stone sarcophagus described extravagantly as a bath, subsequently preserved in the garden

7

The Georges maintain
allegiance to sea bathing:
here, the Prince Regent,
flanked by graceful Brighton
nymphs, is about to enter a
bathing-machine.

as a historic relic and receptacle for ornamental plants instead of royal
backsides. Graduating via sea-water baths at a local establishment, His
Majesty finally came to the supreme moment: his first descent from a
bathing-machine into the ocean of which he was monarch.

Bathing was an operation preferably conducted privately for a man of
George III's unathletic physique and parlous state of health, but his
chances of dipping one royal toe without an audience were, inevitably,
small. More than once his ablutions were trumpeted to the world
with the subtlety of a modern loudspeaker announcement by a blaring
band concealed craftily inside another bathing-machine, waiting to
squawk out a tune he had doubtless long ago come to detest, *God Save
the King*, as soon as his nose poked from the little wheeled coop. No
less than a thousand men allegedly mounted picket duty over Gloucester
Lodge itself, ensuring both that no undesirable person ever got in, and
also that no personally desirable but unkingly urge got the better of
the semi-imprisoned monarch.

The frustrations born of exaggerated and over-acted loyalty to the
crown in the person of King George, when it put aside its robes and
donned bathing-drawers or worse, were vividly recorded in the diary of
the famous novelist Fanny Burney, Second Keeper of the Robes to
Queen Charlotte and a member of the Weymouth holiday parties.

They have dressed out every street with labels, 'God Save the King'. The bathing
machines make it their motto over all their windows, and those bathers that belong
to the royal dippers wear it in bandeaus on their bonnets to go into the sea; and
have it again in large letters round their waists, to encounter the waves. Think of
the surprise of His Majesty when, the first time of his bathing, he had no sooner
popped his royal head under the water than a band of music concealed in a
neighbouring machine struck up *God Save Great George Our King!*

8

Did he pray that God *would* save him — from his own subjects' adulation?

Instinctively, George III sensed what was to become the essence of the seaside as a place for pleasure and relaxation and set less store on pomp and dignified, laughterless perambulations than on simple beach games and the company of small fry. Even the instinct of the railway excursion age, as yet far in the future, and of the motoring era, still further ahead — to aim for reaching the beach half an hour before one left home and waste not an instant on the way — was anticipated by this king who could not get to the seaside fast enough, a road-hog regularly pulling off the considerable feat of reaching Weymouth under four-footed horsepower, changed every ten miles, on the same day that he had left Windsor, having departed at four o'clock in the morning to arrive in time for supper.

> Georgie Porgie,
> Pudden and pie,
> Kissed the girls
> And made them cry.

goes a nursery rhyme sometimes said to refer to this monarch who unashamedly enjoyed his suppers of 'pudden and pie', along with complete wagonloads of provisions trundled down from Windsor in order to overcome the shameless cashing-in of local shopkeepers and growers. But, far from making little girls cry, kind-hearted Georgie Porgie, or Farmer George, was not ashamed publicly to kiss a little commoner girl on Weymouth beach and make her smile again.

Never did neighbourhood gawpers gawp with mouths wider open or jaws lower sagging than when that same child arrived at her own poor cottage door riding like Cinderella in King George's personal carriage behind superb horses, accompanied by a man who might have been a duke, in his fairy-tale coat of velvet and lace and big cocked hat — the King's personal physician, commanded to attend this child found crying on the sands after an attack by stone-throwing boys and rescued by the King himself. It was not the only time that Weymouth would hear good of the third George.

Punch ponders the likelihood of all-year bathing in 1898.

[The *Lancet* advocates taking holidays in Midwinter instead of Midsummer.]
VIEW OF THE SANDS OF ANYWHERE-ON-SEA IF THE SUGGESTION IS ADOPTED. TIME—DECEMBER OR JANUARY.

Emergent Tynemouth in
1839, when emphasis began
to shift from inland spas to
the sea.

Down onto the beach went the King on many other occasions,
lending his presence to simple peasant pleasures and making them, by
example, the 'Done Thing' for every social aspirant of genuine breeding
or upstart pretensions. The Athletic Sports he patronised there in
1798 thus differed little from similar contests staged among the
wealthy when disporting themselves in what they imagined was un-
affected rustic fashion at spas and seaside resorts, hospital fêtes and
charity events, for the next century and a quarter and by office girls on
half-day outings for another quarter century after that:

A Cheese to be rolled down the Hill, prize to whoever stops it.
A pound of tobacco to be grinned for (The frighfull'st Grinner be the Winner).
A hat to be cudgelled for.
Half a Guinea for the best Ass in three heats.
A handsome Hat for the Boy most expert in catching a Roll dipped in Treacle and
suspended by a String.
A leg of Mutton and a gallon of Porter to the winner of a race of a hundred yards in
sacks.
A good Hat to be wrestled for.
Half a Guinea to the rider of an Ass who wins the best three heats by coming in
last.
A Pig for whoever catches him by the Tail.

George III's final Weymouth sojourn came in 1805, but by then the
cult of the seaside was firmly moulded into its now traditional playtime
essentials, and the architectural style of Weymouth was being repeated
all round the coast. By the 1850s it could be already written of
Worthing that 'the rapid rise of this place, from an obscure village
within the memory of man is said to be due to the patronage bestowed
upon it by George III', with the eloquent addition that 'the inns are
excellent, and the modern buildings . . . display considerable taste and
elegance.'

The south coast in particular thanked George III as much as God for
its creation as early as 1840.

Brighton beach: the
modesty hood has arrived —
and so has the
binocular-and-telescope
brigade, hoping to 'see
something'.

The Gentlemen! who pass the morning near the
Ladies Bathing Machines

Since George III introduced the fashion of regularly going to the southern coast for health, London and other doctors have been in the habit of recommending to those who cannot or choose not to go abroad, the same description of residence in all cases of individuals of consumptive habit. The particular spot designated for this purpose has varied from time to time, having extended west and south, farther and farther every eight or ten years; from Weymouth to Sydmouth, from Sydmouth to Exmouth, and so on to Dawlish and Teignmouth, and lastly and now to Torquay.

Three more factors clinched for the people what King George is credited with having begun for the wealthy minority: early legislation making a few modest days' freedom from work a right, such as the 1833 Factory Act, which stipulated that workers under eighteen should enjoy eight annual half days, and the Bank Holidays Act of 1871; gradual adoption by employers of holidays with pay from about 1875 (though as late as the 1920s workers still might be 'stood off' without work or pay at slack periods and be expected to regard this as their 'holiday'); and the growth of railways, opening up travel, formerly the privilege of the exclusive and well-horsed, to Mr and Mrs Everyman and their brood. Almost simultaneously holiday preferences shifted away from spas to seaside watering-places, from health-seeking combined with stylised entertainment in artificial and insincere company towards pleasuring for the boisterous, unhypochondriacal multitude.

Thenceforth Puffing Billy and a day or week at the sea would go together right through to beyond the Second World War, when at last Puffing Billy would cease to puff, breathing instead with bronchial diesel snorts or electrified staccato rattles; when a sudden upsurge of private family motoring would kill the steamers and break the railways' monopoly, overseas holidays would become cheap and available to all, and television would destroy do-it-yourself entertainment.

Just launched at Brighton in about 1900.

That century, approximately from the mid-1830s to the brink of war in 1939, was the heyday of the English seaside, when children were children instead of sophisticated miniature adults; when cockles and mussels contented working-class diners, before barmaids on inflated earnings invaded luxury hotels and over-dressed for dinner; when postcards were naughty instead of outright obscene; when voluminous bodices and bloomers from neck to ankle became as sexy as any scanty bikini, once immersed in all-revealing wetness; when the latest hits came from *Rose Marie* or *Chu Chin Chow* or the happy halls, and pop songs were uninvented; when ships plied pier to pier almost as regularly as trains from station to station, and nobody hurried for a missed bus ('Never mind, dear; there'll be another in a minute' — and there was); when kissers were 'spoons' and lovers were 'loons'; when nine old pence took a couple to the flicks (best stalls) and included a bagful of coconut ice, and a tinny piano tinkled out hurry-music while jerky goodies caught up with gun-toting baddies.

These are the years with which the present volume chiefly concerns itself, intended as a miscellany of delights and sensations, what the butler saw and what Auntie *thought* she saw, of Wakes Weeks and Bank Holidays, charabancs and bathing-machines, rather than a sober chronological social history. It begins, however, where Alice began in Wonderland: at the beginning, when Bournemouth was but a few clumps of bedraggled heather, Blackpool a black, lonely peaty pool, and Southend pier a rude timber jetty stopping a mile short of the sea.

The seaside age is fully developed and so is the age of jokes about 'sarfend on mud'. This one comes from a 1908 issue of *Punch*.

12

2. 'Bournemouth? Never Heard of It!'

The original Mrs Bloomer, inventor of the notorious, daring garments named after her, Bloomers.

> God made the country,
> And man made the town.

But who, George III apart, made the point where they often meet, the seaside; the seaside of bathing-machines and bloomers, Kiss-me-quick hats and rock?

God, certainly; for are we not told that 'The sea is His, and He made it', as well as 'the dry land'? Man continued, by attaching first shacks, then villages to the shore; then cart tracks followed by roads; but it remained for God and man's brain to combine in science before the work of creation was complete, with the discovery that steam, restrained in a boiler that ran on rails, could drive wheels at an unimaginable pace, giving men the nearest thing to wings wherewith to reach the ends of the land, instead of only the ends of their own parishes, for pleasure as well as necessity.

Between the improvement of roads into turnpikes negotiable by carriages and the establishment of the fully developed network of railways the English seaside resort saw its most noticeable growth; from a handful of smugglers' huts under lonely cliffs where Bournemouth was not yet thought of, or gipsies' booths near that bleak black pool on the dreary Lancashire coast, to the Margate of inter-war tripperdom and the Blackpool of Wakes Weeks.

The seventeenth-century British coastline was an inhospitable place in general, and holidays in our modern sense were unknown. Even Sussex, nearest London, was a network of quagmires rather than roads, linking hamlets of ragged barefoot infants, straggle-haired mothers and hay-heaving yokels to a few poor coastal fishing villages. So bad was the terrain as to suggest a direct effect on the inhabitants. Thus Dr John Burton, writing from backward Lewes: 'Why is it that the oxen, the swine, the women, and all the other animals, are so long legged in Sussex? May it be from the difficulty of pulling the feet out of so much mud?' Not until macadamisation, followed by railwayisation, would Sussex loose its feet of clinging clay, except on the royal road to Brighton.

It was another doctor, Dr Russell, who truly set Brighton on the way to becoming 'Doctor Brighton', a tag still used into the twentieth century; merely to climb a hill forty miles inland was standard health practice for the writer's grandmother as a young mother, for her brood to breathe air described as Brighton breezes.

Fishing village; health resort; pleasure place; the middle of these
functions could undoubtedly be attributed to Dr Russell's faith in
Brighthelmstone, pronounced Brighton. When he began practising in
the early eighteenth century, it was a poor neighbour indeed to his
own town of Lewes, but the only commodities it possessed in abundance,
clean air and salt water, could, he believed, become invaluable thera-
peutic aids to city-polluted patients, were they made aware of their
benefits. His treatise of 1750 so persuasively lauded the effects of sea
water taken both internally and externally, notably for glandular
complaints, that it became acknowledged the greatest single factor that
first made Brighton fashionable. Soon Russell himself moved to
'clean and neat' Brighthelmstone, there to practise profitably what he
preached, though not for another century would the famous tag Doctor
Brighton actually be attached to the town. Not for another three
decades would the young Prince of Wales lure healthy instead of ailing
fashion Brightonwards and open its third phase, as the 'gay summit of
pleasure and fashion'. Even then, Dr Russell's part in its meteoric rise
and growth was not overlooked, the man who by prescribing Brighton as
a tonic, also gave a tonic shot to that pallid small fishing village. As was
remarked in 1813: 'At the Old Ship Tavern in Ship Street . . . the
ballroom . . . is large and elegantly furnished, and adorned with an
admirable portrait of Doctor Russell, who is respected by the inhabitants
as the first person that brought Brighton into general repute.'

Not every sleeping beauty of a village had the luck to be wakened by
a prince whose arrival was sufficient to create an entire new town
merely because fashion followed slavish fashion. In the north, at the
opposite extreme, it was the wraggle-taggle gipsies who gave the kiss of
life to a bleak straight Lancashire strand destined to become for Mr and
Mrs Average what Brighton was to Lord and Lady Grandness.

There being little to amuse early strollers along the Fylde coast but throwing pebbles into the sea, looking for shells or wandering by the unprepossessing dark peaty pool which gave Blackpool its ultimate appellation, the simple sideshows, coconut shies and roundabouts erected by Blackpool's eighteenth-century gipsy population to cash in on such leisure-seekers as did find that little-known place quickly attracted enough trade to justify their becoming a regular feature. Few of the thousands patrolling today's Pleasure Beach and Golden Mile consciously link their fortune-tellers, whether genuine or assumed Romany, each claiming unconvincingly to be the only original Gipsy Rose Lee, with the very birth of this celebrated pleasure dome by the sea; but in them is indeed the clue to Blackpool's conception.

Not until the 1760s did one Mrs Whiteside, a Welshwoman married to a Fylde dweller, become the pioneer Blackpool landlady, when she first offered the visitors beginning to arrive in summer lodgings at her modest cottage by the healthy Irish Sea, not far from the namesake black pool. From the start, she set the basic pattern for Blackpool's famous landladies of two following centuries, with simple but appetising North Country cookery in generous helpings, much as modern Mrs Whitesides tempt those who, here more than in almost any other resort, still prefer 'digs' to hotels.

A Mrs Average of about 1880, dressed with her family for a seaside outing; the little 'girl' with the curl down the forehead is in fact a little Victorian boy.

Mrs Whiteside's and the gipsies' Blackpool continued primarily a fishing village, only slowly expanding its visitors' accommodation and adding such amenities as dancing and supping outdoors at a shanty on the clifftops. It needed railways, a late arrival here, to arouse it as Brighton had awakened at least a century earlier; not until 1876 did Blackpool receive its first Royal Charter of Incorporation, the formal birth certificate proclaiming the end of 150 years' gestation from gipsy haunt to full town.

While Lancashire's Mrs Whiteside was cooking for her first season's guests, Brighton showed little more life, 'a small, insignificant place . . . little frequented', harbouring only seven thousand souls. Yet, within twenty seasons, its growth became extraordinarily rapid.' By 1809 'there were upwards of 2000 houses and 12,000 settled inhabitants, and . . . the annual visitors, for the purposes of health and pleasure, amounted to an equal number.' Also expanding was the Sussex resort's reputation for relationships between gay London bucks and warm-hearted local belles; for dashing exaggerated display, as when one Barrymore drove two struggling horses up Mrs Fitzherbert's elegant staircase and enthralled the tattlers by requiring a posse of coachmen and blacksmiths to extricate them; for extravagant regal expenditure, as when the royal princes' birthdays were celebrated with whole roasted oxen and strong beer allegedly running like water and quaffed as freely; for courtly courtship, artificial manners and delicious scandal, played against the exotic background of the astonishing Royal Pavilion, seaside home of the First Gentleman of Europe. What cared

Tiny Dawlish, almost a non-resort in 1839, as yet unawakened by railways.

those fortunate enough — or pretty enough — to catch royal eyes and enter its portals that such men as Cobbett called Prinny's bauble an English Kremlin?

When you see the thing from a distance, you think you see a parcel of cradlespits; . . . take a large Norfolk turnip, cut off the green leaves, leave the stalks nine inches long, tie these round with a string three inches from the top, and put them on the corners of [a] box; then take a considerable number of bulbs of the crown-imperial, the narcissus, the hyacinth, the tulip, the crocus and others; let the leaves of each have sprouts to about an inch, more or less according to the size of the bulb; put all these, pretty promiscuously but pretty thickly, on the top . . . There! That's a Kremlin!

Prinny's Brighton was renowned, too, for splendid public transport — at least two coaches daily — and everlasting promenading of elaborately-groomed pedestrians or ornately-carriaged private families; for theatre, folly and fashion; above all, for the goings-on when Martha Gunn, mistress of the bathing-machines, assisted the briney ablutions of ladies clothed neck to toe in voluminous yet provocatively wet fabrics, while gentlemen dipped from other machines draped from Adam's apple to toenails only in baby-pink natural hide.

How different from such non-rivals as small straightlaced Margate, so many wearisome hours' sailing down Thames by sea-sickly hoy that many never continued but contented themselves with making riverside Gravesend a seaside without the sea. Those who braved Margate for its unusually strong and toning air seem to have clung not to the Regent's new seaside age but the declining spa period with its insistence on etiquette, precedence, correctness of address and daily round of formal stylised pleasures. The notion of paddling the feet and enjoying oneself without thought for appearances surely appeared absurd, if not disgusting, to he who penned *A Picture of Margate* in about 1810.

16

Scarborough in about 1840, one of England's few large resorts of the early Victorian period.

When strangers of respectability arrive at Margate, the Master of Ceremonies, if such persons be not personally known to him, expects an early opportunity of being introduced to them, as such an introduction tends to preserve that order and decorum, so necessary in such a place of mixed resort, and is the means of preventing improper company from coming into the Rooms.

Early nineteenth-century topographers quickly seized on the value of census figures, a very new weapon, in surveying Britain between the Georges' waning and the baby Victoria's first cradled gurgles, materially increasing the value of their impressions. Thus an historic volume in the present writer's ownership paints our seaside resorts of about 1811 in terms we can set unusually clearly against them as they are today. 'East Bourne, which has of late years become a fashionable bathing place . . . situated near the foot of the lofty hill which forms the bold headland of Beachy.' (Nothing speaks volumes: Eastbourne boasts no figures at all.) Or, again, 'This place has of late years been much frequented for the purpose of sea-bathing, but as yet the accommodations which it affords are upon a very limited scale' — all that could be said, in a volume of many hundred pages, of Littlehampton near the time of Waterloo. And, returning eastwards, 'Seaford has of late attracted some visitors during the bathing season; three machines are kept, and hot and cold baths have been erected for their accommodation; . . . 146 houses, 166 families, 847 persons, 68 in agriculture, 62 in trade, manufactures and handicrafts.' Not, let it be noted, in the hotel business. Worthing was already attempting to awaken as the alarm clock of progress clanged; indeed, its eyes were sufficiently open to encourage it into over-ambitiousness.

Worthing has suffered much from the too great eagerness of speculators to profit by the fashionable propensity to frequent watering-places; and though the number of its houses may have greatly increased of late years, yet it is not too much to assert

17

Highlight of Great
Yarmouth's holiday
mornings was the arrival of
the London boat, when
ships sailed 'black with
people'.

that its prosperity has diminished in a like ratio as there are now many more than
can find occupants. Should the people of Worthing have the good sense to abstain
from any new enterprises for a few years, it cannot be doubted that the additional
influx of company attracted by the recent improvements will enable them to repair
the losses occasioned by the error into which they have fallen.

Other coastlines fairly consistently repeated this Sussex pattern during
the opening years of the nineteenth century, usually having one premier
established resort and several medium-sized rivals rising to notice
with new terraces, lodgings, lending libraries and bathing-machines;
while others, today's holiday heavens, were as yet almost undiscovered.
Some once-prosperous sites, recently declined, enjoyed unexpected
revival thanks to those strange fads of bathing and health residence
favoured by rich families, as at Aldeburgh in Suffolk, likewise surveyed
in about 1811.

Till within the last 15-20 years, Aldborough [sic], depopulated and impoverished
by the incroachments of the sea, was hastening to complete decay; but several
families of distinction, wishing for a greater degree of privacy and retirement than
can be enjoyed in a fashionable watering place, having made this town their
summer residence, its appearance has lately been totally changed. To the deep
sands which formerly led to it, have succeeded excellent turnpike roads; instead of
the clay-built cottages which gave the place a mean and squalid appearance, are
now seen many neat and comfortable mansions, the property and occasional retreat
of persons of rank and fortune.

The place boasted '201 houses, 804 inhabitants' besides visitors
(roughly, one modern street) and 'a small market twice a week, on
Wednesday and Saturday, and two annual fairs, on March 1 and May
3'. What a round of non-excitement was life before the word 'train'
entered English dictionaries.

Blackpool: Preston workers' mecca from the earliest days.

Lowestoft, 'commanding an extensive view of the German Ocean' (North Sea), described as 'a remarkably beautiful object' of a township, retained one sad drawback when the seaside was a place to enjoy being ill or semi-ill rather than well; though 'the declivity formerly barren sand' had been 'converted by modern improvements into gardens interspersed with alcoves and summerhouses', the rest of the town hid coyly away from the all-important beach: 'the distance . . . from the water is considered an inconvenience by the invalids who resort to Lowestoft for the benefit of sea-bathing.' Otherwise, admittedly, these shores were 'peculiarly favourable, consisting of a hard sand inter-mingled with shingle, perfectly free from ooze and . . . beds of mud'.

Much would happen in the twenty short years between these surveys of Britain's alternately fashionable and dispirited resorts, according to their patronage, as in 1811, and the 1830s with their

19

expanding populations and disenchantment with the parochialism of bygone ages, almost as if folk tangibly sensed the imminence of practicable family road travel followed by railways, liberating minds as well as bodies. Unusually laggardly though Lancashire would prove railwaywise, the blood of future Wakes began rising in both supervisory and working-class veins directly horse transport reached public service standard.

Very early was set the unwritten law that 'Manchester people have their favourite sea-bath at Southport' while Preston automatically migrated to Blackpool. As an 1840 observer expanded:

To Southport the Manchester factor and artisan — the rich and the 'middling-comfortable' — repair during two months of the year, either for a week or two's residence, or for a mere frolic. At that period one may see the walls of that smokey city [Manchester] placarded with 'Cheap travelling to Southport'; 'Only Five Hours to Southport'; 'Excursion to Southport', and vociferations from a hundred throats to the same effect, are to be heard from the top of every species of vehicle in the principal streets.

Only five hours for all of forty miles; progress, marvellous modern progress!

'No wonder,' added this early Victorian oracle, 'that those who can luckily escape the sootinizing atmosphere of Manchester, to plunge into the "wide, wide sea", there to wash off the black deposits on their skins, should eagerly seize the opportunity of repairing even to such a sea-bathing place as Southport.'

Preston's scrub-weary elbows and calloused fists meanwhile descended in almost frighteningly increasing legions on Blackpool, fortune-telling capital of our coasts, possibly in hopes of hearing that Uncle Bert, last heard of in wildest Saskatchewan forty years before, had left one enough to open that dream of opulent self-supporting prosperity, a boarding-house. The Boswells, gipsy royalty, ruled Blackpool's attractions for quite four decades, joined by other families and such celebrated relations as Sarah Boswell, palmist extraordinary and spiritual matriarch of soothsayers from Lancashire down to Kent until today. Only later would authority remove them to the site of a later and more sophisticated Pleasure Beach, where their caravans and booths, gay with Romany carpentry and paintwork, continued as pre-Tower Blackpool's prime attraction.

Yes, a long jolting road slog by horse brake was worth it, Blackpool being 'much more readily accessible than Southport by a paved road' when Victoria was scarcely crowned.

Whilst Manchester and Preston floated off their workaday grime into the Lancashire waves, saving bathwater, lugging of ewers of hot water and cakes of harsh yellow soap, Newcastle similarly de-grimed and deodorised its person and uplifted its factory-oppressed soul on the opposite side of England. The muddiest waves were heaven to refugees from back-to-back housing where brackish unwholesome water spurted from street installations, and oval tin baths in the kitchen, if one cleansed at all,

Blackpool Tower soon became famous enough to stand as an international measurement of height. In this postcard of about 1908 the Tower is compared with the now demolished Singer Building in New York.

sufficed for father, mother and children in succession on Friday bath-night. In this vein the eye of 1840 alighted on Tynemouth where many variously sized sharp and swarthy rocks . . . render sea bathing altogether an operation requiring caution; yet here upon these sands, within this contracted space, on which I espied a few straggling bathing machines, do the Newcastle people and others from the neighbourhood repair, for the luxury of washing off with muddy sea water the sooty layers deposited on their skins during the lengthened winter season.

Exclaimed this visitor, having toured literally every British seaside resort then extant: 'I never saw anything less inviting, or more discouraging for a bather.' What would be his conclusions now, of Tynemouth's 'aspect of poverty' changed by time?

21

Where Blackpool led, other resorts followed in pursuit of pleasure. Great Yarmouth's flag-decked skeletal tower in about 1918.

A Bible Class poses in pillboxes by the bathing-machines of 1908.

Weymouth apart, it became generally clear halfway through the nineteenth century which were to be the great resorts and how their characters differed: Brighton ('of late years . . . struggling to escape from the sea . . . creeping up inland'); Torquay, the expensive consumptives' retreat into gloom before the tomb ('frequent tolling of the funeral bell, as every one of 44 patients of condition arrived at Torquay had died, principally during the first 2 quarters of the year . . . awful and thrilling to the rest, who were trembling on the verge of their graves with symptoms of the same devouring malady'); and Blackpool at the hearty, let's-be-matey opposite extreme in health, outlook, breeding and cash resources alike. Only one major resort remained unformed, some five miles of golden south coast seafront, nowadays famous for Knightsbridge-standard stores, lavish entertainment, cultural amenities and literally innumerable fine hotels, which few bathers ever mentioned, for a simple reason — it barely existed.

So insignificant was this huddle of cottages and lodgings adopted by handfuls of pioneer seekers of almost cloistral sequestration that such peasantry as a literary traveller of 1839 met on the wild, highwayman-infested heaths where it lay considered 'the existence of the incipient colony' not worth mentioning. Maps marked the same road either 'To 'Christchurch' or 'To Poole', placing not even a dot, let alone a name, to mark the village, 'albeit the identical road passed through it'. Neither did officialdom acknowledge primitive Bourne, the future Bournemouth; no figures are extractable from early census returns, the few inhabitants being added to Poole or Christchurch. The beaches were bare but for smugglers' shacks, mementoes of the notorious

Sandcastle competition, 1900—something gayer than invalids' Bournemouth.

Hawkhurst and Gulliver gangs of brandy-running days, and china clay workings serving the Potteries before the advent, about 1835, of such superb public entertainments, appropriate to a rising young resort, as one bathing-machine, a lending library and the first prophetic outbreak of sham chalets and mock-Italian villas. 'The place is entirely occupied by invalids suffering from chest complaints, and every lodging is taken during the course of February,' a Victorian doctor concluded, adding that even those whose final Bourne lodging-place was a grave reflected no blame on the village, being 'only . . . those patients who had been sent . . . in a hopeless state'.

Something gayer than an invalids' Bournemouth stirred in visionary minds before the century's halfway mark. This tiny sea-nook in a superb setting of heath, pine and cliffs overlooking a glittering bay could become as magnetic to the quick as to the half-dead, given such common amenities as shops (in 1839 Bourne possessed not even one, 'tradesmen [being] in the habit of calling for orders and with supplies every day' from Poole) and public walks. What elegant crescents could adorn those artistic natural slopes above the Bourne stream, following under its 'insignificant wooden bridge' directly onto the beach where a pier ought to be, through a 'vale [consisting] of a narrow belt of peat earth lying over sand, on which a few miserable sheep are allowed to feed, or a scanty, coarse grass is cut'. That scrubby vale could in the imagination become 'a regular promenade garden all the way, with parterres and beds of flowers by the sides of the brook . . . the prettiest thing in England'. And it did, perhaps half a century onwards, as Bournemouth's famous Central Gardens.

23

Railways both killed this second seaside period of ozone-therapy and created its third era, that of pleasure; killed the world of sedate bath-chaired gouty colonels and peevish baronets' wives and facilitated that occupation abhorred by the more pious of our great-grandfathers, 'pleasuring'.

Ever more companies piled coal into bunkers, laid rails and touted for custom with enthusiastic advertising of spartan but cheap trains. The first giant excursion train gasped into Brighton barely two and a half hours after leaving London, and up north the name of Cook appeared.

Thomas Cook, whose empire descended from experimental, fully-booked special trains carrying supporters across country to temperance rallies, had a Fylde counterpart thenceforth known simply as Cook of Blackpool. The latter is credited, shortly after the local line's opening, with introducing cheap returns from other Lancashire towns for pleasure purposes, return to the home station to be made the same day, thus materially helping Blackpool to establish its permanent reputation as a day trippers' resort. Soon excursions were sanctioned on Sundays, the only free day for most labourers, a splendid peg on which Fylde country clergy could hang endless sermons of damnation against 'swift and safe excursions to Hell'. But no sermoniser could reverse what Cook of Blackpool and the railway directors had consolidated, an inevitable progression towards the first rock shop, first tram, first pier and the first girders of a tower, rearing ever higher, that must have engendered something of the awe experienced aeons before by witnesses of the building of another monstrous tower, Babel.

Oh! century of contrasts! Adolescent Blackpool and newborn Bournemouth; royal Brighton and embryonic Bexhill, 'a parish in the Rape of Hastings, county of Sussex, remarkable for its various chalybeate springs', all that could be gazetteered of that future suburbia-on-sea as late as 1851.

Oh! century of change, putting to permanent flight the genteelly ailing carriage folk of Torquay; at least partially loosening strangulating stays, a significant factor in reducing tuberculosis, and introducing something faintly resembling leisure garb, thus changing the function of lodgings from semi-mortuaries of wealthy coughers into the happier boarding-houses and 'digs' beloved of lower classes and trade; raising skirts ankle high for paddling; multiplying bathing-machines in thousands; making bloomers respectable when wet with sea water, if not dry; bringing train-born multitudes to Skegness and Scarborough, Merry Margate and awakening Southend, to see what the butler saw. Most could barely afford a week, often no more than a day trip, instead of the Georgian consumptive's leisurely season; but into those hours they crammed more enjoyment than any languishing penny-romance heroine dreamed was either possible or decent.

They made the seaside seasidey.

Ozone-therapy: taking the air with dignity at Herne Bay in about 1911.

Tripper take-over: the charabanc generation arrives.

25

3. 'Electric Light in All Rooms'

Hotel, diggings or some alternative between? That was the holiday question, assuming one could afford holidays at all.

Between about 1830 and 1930 the choice was as wide as the financial gulf between wealth, when the rich were more flamboyantly rich than at almost any other period, and poverty, when the poor were poor to a degree unknown today.

Social background as well as money governed that choice. A boilerhand, given an unexpected windfall on the 'gees', still automatically booked diggings, the universal digs, conscious that sampling higher life would bring embarrassment, not pleasure. Digs it had always been, and Ma Brown's villa it would be that year too.

Coastal Britain, set on its commercial feet by roads and railways, could house satisfactorily anyone from Major Harrison-Hodson, peevishly complaining in his gilded Torquay palace that some dashed nuisance of a war prevented his usual foreign sojourn, to Pa Bloggs, scrimping and saving all year to rear six children and a wife on £3 a week, find 12s 6d (62½p) rent, pay a penny weekly insurance for eventual burial of Ma — everyone talked before the children of death insurance when such monetary disasters could only be weathered by lifelong forethought — and still manage a seaside week for the family, if only once in three years. Downwards ran the list of possibilities: grandest palace hotel; hydro; first-class hotel; middling hotel; smaller private hotel; boarding establishment (subtly more respectable than a boarding-house); digs, in private or semi-private houses; hired apartments, if well off; the same, referred to as rooms, if poorer; Christian guest-house; temperance hotel; commercial inn; or sponging on a cousin's sister who let one room two miles outside Clacton, proportionately cheaply.

The word hotel is believed to have first been used in England towards the onset of the seaside age, not far inland from Exmouth, when in 1770 the still extant Royal Clarence at Exeter so called itself. Being the sole example, it was known only as The Hotel, later the Hotel in the Churchyard, from its site on the edge of the cathedral close.

Close behind the word hotel came the expressions Grand Hotel; Palm Court; terrace tearoom; gracious living — particularly before railways, when only the grandest in breeding could afford to sojourn at spas or socially acceptable resorts. Such was Scarborough in 1740, combined resort and spa, when 'earls, marquesses and dukes were as

Previous pages: holiday time in 1873. The bedlam of a crowded beach makes a vivid contrast with the tiny resorts of a few decades earlier.

28

Assembled guests in the garden of a Broadstairs establishment pose at the end of their holiday.

thick . . . as berries are on hedges', brought by splendid private carriages, coats of arms emblazoned on their polished panels, with toppered coachmen and curled little Misses in tow, all expecting a bowing-and-scraping welcome while an additional wagonette of servants and baggage rumbled round the back. How pointed was the contrast between masters' front suites and vassals' back or mews quarters, as marked as that between wooden-bunked steerage dormitories, heavily disinfected of necessity, and the astonishing floating Adam drawing-rooms of First Class at sea.

Servants at Bournemouth's earliest top-class hotel were thus unusually lucky when it was written in about 1839 that

the second storey bedrooms, destined for servants, are a 'manque' floor, with windows like holes and rooms small and low — too good for servants, for they enjoy the finest views imaginable — too bad for masters, as to accommodation . . . besides, to have rattling servants . . . stamping their heavy tread immediately over the heads of their masters and mistresses is a most objectionable arrangement; menservants should never be in the same 'corps de logis' with their masters, but [be] made to occupy separate outbuildings, at all great hotels.

Palace; Imperial; Grand: every pretending resort built itself one example of the best of the best, beyond the dreams of perhaps 95 per cent of visitors, condemned only to stare bashfully past the impressive admiral of a commissionaire, daily extricating furred ladies and tailored gentlemen from carriages, or the earliest snob-appeal motorcars, into the only visible section of the carpeted and leather-chaired vestibule, and to wonder how it felt to be rich.

29

Even on the beach, formal dress remained the rule in pre-car England.

Only that exclusive 5 per cent actually knew what advertisements meant by 'Every Accommodation for comfort' in the heyday of ostentation: 'Electrically lighted; mechanically ventilated; hydraulic lifts; excellent cuisine; moderate charges; personally patronised by their Majesties the King and Queen, Their Royal Highnesses the Prince and Princess of Wales and many other Royal and Distinguished visitors'.

Royal patronage guaranteed that England's marquesses and field-marshals followed, demanding evidence of the luxury they paid for even before seeing their hotel, as at Colwyn Bay in 1907: 'Porters in scarlet livery attend all trains.'

'Motor Garage' appeared in hotel blandishments directly the first car drew a gaping crowd, alongside such gentlemanly essentials as 'reading, smoking and billiards rooms' and that loudest crow of advertising triumph early in the twentieth century, 'Electric Light in ALL Rooms'. Some went better, with 'Motor Garage and Inspection Pit' — for use by the chauffeur and mechanic, naturally: an owner never got himself greasy.

In sanitation, likewise, the best led the rest, charging accordingly. As early as about 1906, indeed, this trend was so established as to percolate down to boarding establishment level in Eastbourne, which prided itself on being the first resort to establish formal sanitary

30

Good class, if not grand: the ladies pose during a Bible Class holiday.

certification, a trend indicated in 'The sanitary arrangements in this establishment are PERFECT, having the Certificate granted by the Medical Officer of Health for the borough' and, later, 'The organic purity of the water is unimpeachable.' Truly nothing is new. Yesterday, it was hygiene regulations; today additional custom is lured by fire safety certificates.

The nearer disaster loomed, the more extravagantly some lived, as if sensing that nothing lasts. Even the Grand was a comedown on leaving a hundred-room mansion behind; only another mansion offered the style to which centuries' old ancestries had accustomed them. Thus a mountain resort near Llandudno in Ward Lock's Red Guide for 1913 lures the shootin' huntin' fishin' gentleman; 'Resembles a Good Country House; in connection with the Hotel, 20,000 acres Really Good Rough Shooting, Grouse, Pheasants etc. Keepers and Dogs provided. Good Salmon and Trout Fishing.' Plenty of room here for retinues of servants from the Big House at home and piles of brass-studded and leather-bonded trunks whose makers boasted that they offered 'quality with economy' yet charged all of thirty shillings (£1.50) for the small size and nearly £2 for a massive cabin trunk holding a lady's entire wardrobe.

When it materialised, war only interrupted Grand Hotel life. Soon after 1918 Scarborough, grander than ever, offered 'a mansion, Tudor

31

Dance orchestra of about 1925 of the type resident in many grander hotels. Note the 'cello (held like a double bass), never seen in dance groups today.

and Baronial' where ladies paid baronial prices to be called Madam in suitably toned voices: 'Staff an object lesson in courtesy'. A rival Grand succinctly called itself merely 'The best equipped and most luxurious hotel in all the West'.

Even luxury had degrees, as in the ballroom in the socially conscious 1930s, golden age of live unvocalised dance music. Never a dance *band* for the Grand (*that* was hired by the night, for dancing alone, receptions and weddings) but a permanently resident professional dance *orchestra*, correctly balanced between wind, percussion and strings — a 'cello has virtually never been seen in dance ensembles since — white-tied, professionaly mannered, with no beermugs under the piano (which four-piece bands indulged in), announced by a politely humorous Master of Ceremonies. Their duties also included elaborate banquets and dinner-dances, providing politely suitable (that is, 'refeened') interlude melody between dancing or as conversation background, whilst jewelled Mamas incited eligible daughters to 'sparkle, dear, sparkle' and catch a man with an establishment, of which to become mistress.

Comparable halls of grandeur were the hydros, whose patrons' holidaymaking, far removed from vulgar beach fun, was combined with expensive medical attention to only semi-incapacitating ills; overlappings of spa kursaal, hotel, nursing home and physiotherapy department, at hydro prices. A Wessex announcement (from the Weymouth Guide of 1906) typifies high hydro life: 'Combining the home comforts and curative advantages of an up-to-date Hydro with the conveniences of a First Class Hotel and excellent cuisine . . . complete installation of electric baths, light treatment, high frequency and vibratory massage, so efficacious in the treatment of rheumatism, gout, neuritis etc., needle-spray, douche and Nauheim baths; physician in attendance'. The difference between dry salty air and foggy inland

Dance band of about 1928,
led by the author's father.
The instrumentation differs
markedly from that of
modern ensembles.

dampness was not yet entirely accepted: 'On medical advice, this
Hotel was built 200ft above the sea, to safeguard against the wet
atmosphere found near breaking seas, so dangerous to rheumatism.'

Clean air, however, had long been appreciated for restoring aristocratic
interiors oppressed by long seasons of *soirées* as much as working-class
lungs polluted by factory grime.Convincing potential long-term residents
of a town's climatic advantages was important, hence much publicity
of the celebrated Swanage Herring Incident, here recounted in about
1905, again from an historic Red Guide.

Invalids . . . used to the soft climates of Bournemouth and Falmouth would find
Dorset air a bracing tonic. The medical profession is realising that a mild climate
with no brisk or invigorating qualities is not the most to be desired from the
standpoint of health. The 'Herring Incident' at Swanage is so well known that we
almost hesitate to repeat it here. At the same time, an absolute proof of the purity
of the air, even if demonstrated by the aid of a common herring, is of value . . . . We
may explain that a herring, fresh from the ocean, was hung up on Durlston Head,
and there left, its condition being carefully noted from time to time. The original
weight was a little over half a pound. After being exposed for two years and five
months, the fish was taken down and found to be only one and one third ounces in
weight — but quite wholesome.

How much more, then, could Swanage do for wheezing man than
for a dead herring?

First-class, but not grand, hotels again led every improvement
seasons ahead of establishments at boarding-house level: jug-and-basin
to hot-and-cold; gas to 'Electric light in ALL rooms'; stairs to lifts;
stabling to garaging; pumps to taps. 'One important article of diet,
water, is indifferent at Brighton', someone wrote from there about
1839; 'it deposits a reddish sand and is in colour dingy. It lathers
tolerably well with soap, but leaves the skin rough . . . In some of the

33

streets there are pumps for public use, but their water is hard.' His hotel water flowed from the same company, but at least it looked better, presented in the latest patterned jug.

Innovations, conversely, could also frighten away valued clientele of the diehard variety, mainstay of expensive hotels' income. It paid to cater for old ways as well as new, carriages as well as noisy new cars. Lynton in Devon affords a good instance in 1919 with 'Electric light throughout . . . 100 horses kept for driving and hunting . . . motor garage'.

Afternoon tea became the most social, if not the most gastronomic, daily ceremony during the 1920s; *thé-dansant* in leading hotels, to a reduced section of the resident orchestra, whilst 'spoons' canoodled behind potted palms at corner tables, softly lit. High living had progressed far since consumptive coffee-room patrons grumbled in 1839 at Torquay of 'the injudicious absurdity of introducing large argand burners of gaslight'.

They felt far from 'benefited', by 'the inhibition of so vitiated an atmosphere', wherein at least one fainted and 'the atmosphere was indeed so oppressive' that the few left, on a doctor's suggestion, had 'the gaslights extinguished and candles introduced instead'.

Eight decades on from Torquay by gaslight, a top hotel could be expected to offer all creature comforts. A gracious penny to ragged local child beggars cannily manning the outside pavements adequately salved ladies' consciences for occupying 'luxurious suites with private bathroom and lavatory complete' and dining daintily on 'milk, butter, cream and eggs from own cows and fowls', or inhabiting, at the same resort, a palace proclaimed 'The Acme of Luxurious Comfort and Artistic Refinement'. Like a hat in a Bond Street milliner's, the Acme displayed nothing so vulgar as its tariff, beyond the comment 'Brochure Free: GREATLY EXCEEDS ALL EXPECTATIONS'. The brochure, or the hotel? Both, presumably.

Even imagining its likely prices were beyond ordinary folk, flipping past the Grands and Imperials in holiday guides towards the boarding-house section. Who could possibly pay at, say, Llandudno, 'Room 5s to 7/6; breakfast or lunch 2/6; tea 1s; dinner 4/6; boarding 9s day, 63s a week; 20s weekend'? Respectable boarding-houses did guests proud, less ostentatiously, on 13s (65p) for a three-day weekend. At a typical temperance hotel, bodies could be kept together with reasonable food, if souls were undefiled by alcohol, on 'Room 1s 6d a day; breakfast 1s 6d; lunch 1s; tea 6d; dinner 1s 6d; boarding 4s daily; 12s weekend'. Because many could not afford a full week, weekend terms were a familiar feature of early twentieth-century advertising.

Comforting is the realisation that even the wealthy had inflation problems as far back as 1906, when there appeared in the Red Guide for Weymouth such wording as:

'Darkroom for photography' became a favourite boarding establishment lure. Or you could go to the High Street chemist, here charging all of 1½d (less than 1p) a print.

We give below a list of principal hotels and boarding houses in South Dorset; the tariffs quoted were supplied by the respective proprietors, but are, of course, liable to alteration. A postcard to any of the hotels, stating requirements and asking for a tariff card, will invariably meet with a quick response.

35

The worst trap, rare in modern holiday literature, was individual services itemised so that they appeared cheap but in reality totalled double normal terms if added to the bill at each day's whim; 'breakfast 2s; lunch 2/6; dinner 3/6; tea 1s; attendance 1s 6d; room 3/6' sounded moderate in about 1918 but totalled 14s (70p) daily compared with all-in terms of only 9 shillings.

As early as 1840 Blackpool represented most expanding resorts, in that 'the principal places for residence are the hotels . . . to suit every class of person' and that the 'class of person' attracted like-minded fellows, setting each category's characteristic clientele. Thus Victorian Blackpool demonstrates the point in two rivals, 'the Capulets and Montagues, red and white roses'; the one 'decorous and stately where the consuming classes, like the articles to be consumed, are of a different and better order, although the charge at each place differs only by sixpence' and the other less select, where hungry hoards 'burst mob-fashion into the dining room . . . such a motley of honest-looking people, men, women and children . . . it has never been my fortune to meet under the circumstances in such numbers before — 50 or 60 in all,' wrote a professional man lodged uneasily there; 'methinks the highest in rank . . . might have been an ironfounder from near Bradford or Halifax, or a retired wine merchant from Liverpool.' Staff duly matched this uninhibited Belshazzar's feast.

About a dozen chambermaids acted as waiters, and there was not a vestige of a manservant . . . . It fell to my lot to dissect the chickens for the ladies. Abundance of meat and sauce seemed to be the desirable thing . . . the meal was appalling, and the serious and busy manner in which every hand and mouth seemed to be at work during the first ten minutes . . . plainly showed how palatable was the fare, and how heady the sea air and the sea bathing of Blackpool.

Good air, unpretentious company, good grub; boarding-house essentials were already ingrained.

For every hotel built, as seasides boomed, twenty roads of identical terraced houses burgeoned, holiday housing for Everyman. Villages became towns in decades, as when Prinny's Brighthelmstone became multiplying Brighton; when Victoria's adoption of Osborne made the Isle of Wight popular enough to attract 'whole fleets of paddle steamers from Southampton . . . carrying cargoes of idlers and loungers', or, up north, in the language of 1810: 'The busy occupation of the masons at once bespoke the thriving condition of the place [Blackpool]; an increase of building was taking place to the South, and a new colony of visitors and bathers is establishing itself there, under the appellation of South Blackpool', the incubation of suburbia-on-sea, plague and spoiler also of the south coast.

Consistency of style prevailed thenceforth, from Blackpool to Brighthelmstone; what posterity terms typical Georgian/Victorian architecture. 'The streets and buildings eastwards of The Steyne are all of modern erection,' commented an 1813 Brighton scribe;

Guests pose with dignity on the steps of a better-class boarding establishment in about 1903.

Marine Parade, St James' Street, High Street, Edward Street, the New Steyne, the Royal Crescent. The last-mentioned range, composed of lodging-houses, is one of the greatest ornaments of Brighton . . . . It must certainly have been with a view to encourage the gratification of a little harmless curiosity, that the builder furnished all these houses with bow windows.

Thirty years on, Hastings similarly sprouted monotonous terraces, Victorian manner: 'three apartments on each floor, the rooms in front, as seems to be the mania of the place, having bow windows and balcony'. Weymouth's terraces appeared equally uniform: 'Mrs Clarke's boarding house is in great vogue . . . because many people will always be found who prefer a gregarious to a solitary life' — moderately-placed trade, hard-saving working girls, London suburbians and Birmingham side-streeters.

'Lodging and boarding houses are of three classes, and at all of them four meals are allowed; the respective prices are 4s 6d; 5s 6d; and 6s 6d a day,' calculated an exhaustive 1839 topographer. Definite differences corresponded to each price; downright rowdy at 4s 6d, uninhibited but not 'a rough lot' at 5s 6d, moderately sedate at 6s 6d, nearer boarding establishment than boarding-house.

A select boarding establishment was operated by ladylike widows or Misses ('The Misses Holland, Proprietresses'); made Ethel M. Dell or her like available, according to generation; advertised 'choir parties catered for' and grew aspidistras atop the piano kept in tune for the

37

said outings, plus residents' sing-songs; and emphasised 'Highest of References in Visitors' Book'. Guests spoke of 'My holiday', instead of the 4s 6d grade 'Me 'ollerdee'. Suitable, Good Class and Respectable was the company; none felt ashamed to display the almost statutory groups wherein all assembled with dignity on the front steps, solemnly watching the photographic birdie said to lurk under the operator's funereal black cloth; nor the ladies-only photographs posed in the parlour to show best hairstyles and dresses advantageously, unsmiling because the required long exposure caused embarrassing facial tics in tensed muscles.

Boarding-house life, by contrast, is epitomised for posterity, possibly unfairly, by the traditional music-hall landlady, arms akimbo, gimlet eye skinned for evidence of 'goings-on', running her house on inexpensive husband-power, two 'kept' daughters and one slavey-cum-waitress required between bed-making and serving to polish industriously with Ready-o ('Green for Brass; Yellow for Aluminium; Rouge for Silver; Mirror for Glass'), and expected like the said cloth to 'do the work until worn to a shred'. The front door was bolted sharp at eleven. Guests ate at set times or went without; took no unauthorised and unpaid baths; brought no outside pals to their rooms; vacated rooms during beach hours; and were made painfully aware of that certain ominous word which inspires accommodation advertisers, even to this day, to insert the phrase 'No Restrictions' into advertisements.

Boarding-house life was the natural habitat of Uncle Bert, talking with mouth stuffed with kippers, and Aunt Mavis, bashing with happy vulgarity and fistfuls of the wrong notes musicians term dominoes on the joanna, while Pa led favourite songs of the halls or degenerate versions of vaguely familiar Good-Class ballads, few as printable as *Land of Hope and Glory* reduced to;

> Land of soap and water,
> Mother, wash thou me . . .

or *Come Into the Garden, Maud* rehashed into 'Come into the garden mud'.

Midweek, a distinct female bias became noticeable, because hard-working Pa's foundry wage barely financed the wife and kids for a week at Margate; he himself could afford no lengthy break. No work, no pay was the common rule. Pa could only join them for the final happy weekend; such legions of weekending Pas, Margate-or Southend-bound, used one timetabled Thames steamer as to bestow its identifying tag, Husbands' Boat or Fathers' Boat.

At Christian guest-houses ('Three minutes churches . . . opposite Baptist chapel'), commonest in Wales, parlour pianos were for hymn-singing, inspiringly beautiful here where voices instinctively slip into full harmony; relaxing refuges within but prime targets for urchins staring without. Few children could resist the spectacle of twenty

38

An unusual amateur snapshot of the heavily-furnished interior of typical 'diggings' in 1929.

adults sitting in a circle reading the Psalms round, verse by verse, as in Sunday School; nor bawling back street versions of standard hymns, like the classic:

> Blessed Insurance
> The money is mine . . .

or their favourite skit on meetings and preachings:

> Dearly beloved brethren, don't you think it is a sin,
> That when you peel potatoes, you throw away the skin?
> For skin feeds pigs; and pigs feed you;
> Dearly beloved brethren, isn't this quite true?

Or what lad failed to notice that one Christian establishment actually called itself, in large letters, Parson's?

Diggings or digs comprised chiefly private lettings in family houses taking handfuls of summer guests to supplement their incomes. The landlady often took genuine interest in such folk as a young secretary, using her annual week to ponder finally and alone the answer to a suitor's wooing; did not prudishly refuse the unheralded arrival of the same impatient suitor, beyond ensuring their rooms were at opposite corners of the landing; but answered 'Yes, I've kept an eye on them!' when in turn his parents and sister also turned up, ostensibly on a day out, ingenuously enquiring 'Have they been good children?'

Landladies' fisherman husbands became good temporary fathers to such girl guests, possibly taking them out to catch their own breakfasts. Sons cheerfully saved taxi fares by running two girls and four large portmanteaux by open tourer to Ryde pier, mainland bound. Both showed interest in a young couple's day out, yet discreetly left them alone in a parlour heavy with striped wallpaper and black-framed portraits.

But, naturally, there were digs *and* digs. The cheapest meant a house's meanest room, furnished with sagging mattresses and rotting curtains 'you could shoot peas through', as the saying went. Poor, for the poorest, but doing invaluable social service in giving impecunious Battersea a few breaths of ozone, even by sleeping four in a bed, continuing the familiar home process embodied in another favourite saying, 'when Mother turns, we all turn.'

39

The car-owning son of a house runs two young ladies, London-bound, back to Ryde pier in 1929; landladies' families acted as combined waiters, porters, cooks and commissionaires.

Modern holiday flats had precursors in rented houses, definitely outside diggings class. Taking a house, by about 1800, was fashionable, as at Worthing, made acceptable by a princess, where 'several of the new streets [were] composed of houses sufficiently extensive and elegant to accommodate the first families in the Kingdom'. At Torquay in 1839 'a detached villa . . . occupied by the family of a noble Earl was let at 10 guineas a week; and they will not let such houses for a shorter term than six months.' In the same year at Scarborough 'a large house near the cliff edge let for 13 guineas during the season.'

Semi-permanent hotel living was marginally cheaper, concluded a Victorian author-doctor of Torquay. 'A family . . . with four daughters and suitable attendants resided here upwards of a year, or two winter seasons, and found their bills to amount to something like a quarter less than in London'; even so, it set Papa back 'a dinner for 3s 6d; tea for 1s 9d; and a bedroom for 2s', big money when the latter two shillings was a London docker's daily pay.

Happily, three groups of seasiders seen between about 1900 and 1930 are rarer today: convalescents, war-wounded and charity children. Peacetime convalescent homes meant legions of paid companions pushing Bath chairs, but during the First World War, many hotels, being half empty, became additional convalescent homes for men repatriated to Blighty minus limbs but alive, to be fed up on special rations, bedded on feathers instead of trench mud, and coddled by waitresses whose motives were not solely patriotic. Those bitter years were sometimes more tellingly embodied in a small child's message to his soldier father than in skilled journalism. Thus penned eleven-year-old Noel on a patriotic postcard of 1919 in the aptly named Convalescent Series: 'Dear Daddy. The front wheel of my bicycle has gone wrong . . . *please* come home and mend it soon.'

Baby travelled by mailcart, precursor of the pram; this picture shows an unusual twin mailcart from about 1905.

Post-Great War orphans' outing organised by the British Legion. Holiday advertising has already crept back onto the 'bus sides.

Noel was lucky. Daddy *did* return to mend bicycles and see his son also serve his monarch in a second holocaust. But thousands of Daddies never returned, explaining a characteristic change of slant in charity appeals to the consciences of those able to thumb through holiday guides. Before 1914 it was usually slum children or broken-down missionaries:

WHAT PUTS THE CITY MISSIONARY OUT OF REPAIR?
1.   The places he must spend his working hours in.
2.   The awful scenes he must witness every day.
3.   The vitiated air he must inbreathe.
4.   The terrible poverty and sickness he sees.

WHAT IS THE REMEDY?
A fortnight at the seaside . . . £2.10s. will provide a free holiday for a missionary for a fortnight.

But different charity trippers characterised the early 1920s, whole convoys of hard-tyred, open-topped buses crammed with war orphans — those whose Daddies would never again repair damaged toys — shepherded by the British Legion and other service organisations, bound for country and sea. Normal travel was also picking up; photographs of these Legion outings clearly show buses carrying large holiday advertisements for Devon and Cornwall. After about 1930, war orphans having grown into wage-earners, the charity section of the sandcastle army reverted to parties from slums and orphanages. 'Many thousands of Poor and Crippled Children would like to have the same privilege as yourself and to ENJOY A HOLIDAY at the SEASIDE or in the GREEN FIELDS,' appealed the famous Shaftesbury Society and Ragged School Union in about 1930; 'ONE GUINEA will pay for a whole Fortnight.'

41

'SUNSHINE IN A £5 NOTE' the Church Army repeated; 'a poor mother and three children can be taken from overcrowded slums for a glorious fortnight at the sea for £5' in Fresh Air Homes. Right to the brink of the Second World War enough poor existed to prompt the Salvation Army into such appeals as: 'From squalid slum to healthy sunshine. This summer hundreds of slum mothers and children will be given a fortnight's holiday by the sea . . . and thousands of needy children will be given a day in the country in a motor-coach, two wholesome meals, and a substantial toy as a memento.'

'A break that mends lives', was this thing modernism takes for granted, a summer holiday. Who cared if better-heeled taunters chanted 'Charity child', when they literally had the time of their lives?

Knifelike the Second World War sliced apart the old society of rich, middle class, trade and poor, redistributing wealth after 1945; the so-called affluent society rose, workers on formerly middle class pay, while the welfare state virtually eliminated true poverty.

Holidays, correspondingly, changed character; charity holidays diminished, except for local council pensioners' schemes; the Grand Tour became coach tripping for factory girls; cruising opened up to hard-saving office workers; boarding-houses increasingly shared trade with holiday camps.

The latter, however, span both phases, pre- and post-war. They were the last new holiday development before 1939.

Only late in the 1930s, as more people became entitled to paid holidays, were businessmen convinced that pleasure could become a mass trade commodity — the holiday industry, as today terms it. Initially, holiday camps were activity holidays, aimed at fairly cultivated clients, centred on drama, bird-watching or nature study, but soon the concept changed to chalets grouped around a communal dining-room and dance-hall, where the expression, 'Smile, damn you, smile' was born.

Thus ducal Georgian rented mansions led to working-class holiday camps, within roughly the same period that turnpikes led to the climax of day trips for multitudes by train, who swelled every resort's seasonal population severalfold. The trippers were the most happy-go-lucky, their daring gradually changing ideas of public decency from a bathing-machine wheel-deep in water via descent at the waves' edge and a traditional machine-cum-chalet on steps at the rear of the beach to hired flimsy tents and, finally, struggling into hired trunks at a bob a day on the beach under a discreetly-held towel.

4. What the Butler Saw

Who created Britain's first landing stage? Doubtless, some prehistoric man, waiting for a friend to give him a lift across a creek by hollowed-out log, who was inspired to throw timbers onto shoreline mud to ease his embarkation. Before the Romans, Britons built wooden huts on stilts above mire, as at Glastonbury lake villages, anticipating pier pavilions on nests of girders. But piers and jetties in a modern sense date chiefy from Tudor times, as regular passenger traffic by water, at definite fares, often easier than over rutted roads, increased, as down the Thames to emergent Southend or across the Mersey to where is now New Brighton.

Mersey ferrying was a bone-shaking business when Daniel Defoe sampled it in about 1720, reporting:

We land on flat shore on the other side . . . to ride through the water for some length, not on horseback but on the shoulders of some honest Lancashire clown, who comes knee deep to the boat's side to truss you up, and then runs away with you as nimbly as you desire to ride, unless his trot were easier; for I was shaken by him that I had the luck to be carry'd by, more than I cared for, and much worse than a hard-trotting horse.

Small wonder, then, that the Isle of Wight was virtually unknown to mainlanders until, in 1813, Ryde built itself England's second longest pier. Being rowed over from ships anchored at an offshore mudbank, lifted out like a side of undignified beef and carried ashore piggy-back like Defoe was not Everyman's idea of holiday arrival.

Nor would Southend, notorious for long periods of low water, become Southend whilst the landfall was as described in about 1839:

The wooden jetty at present in existence, and the only convenient place people have to land upon, extends only to about half a mile, and is always left dry at low tide. It is then followed out by a line of shingle, projecting perhaps a quarter mile farther, and called The Hard. Then follows a space of clear water, even at low tide, which divides the termination of The Hard from a cluster of piles in the sea called The Mount, on which a hut is built.

At The Mount, over a mile out, steamers landed passengers to be ferried over the shallows to the beginning of The Hard, then to trudge to the mud-marooned jetty. It was a hard, squelching plod for women in tight boots and billowing bombazine skirts hauling grizzling infants through oozing shingle and for husbands loaded with hampers.

43

"JUSTICE FOR WOMEN!" OR, THE DECLINE OF CHIVALRY.

A Tragedy of the North Sea.

Seaside high jinks seen through *Punch*'s eye in 1908.

Officialdom, inevitably, though conscious that Southend's proximity to London automatically ensured prosperity from the sea-bathing craze, which must expand umpteenfold given adequate landing facilities, bumbled on so fruitlessly about extending the jetty that, after ten years, it still seemed that 'there is as little probability as ever that this much desired continuation will ever be accomplished'; Southend, however, did ultimately acquire its world-famous pier, as must every other bathing place knowing that steamer traffic was its financial life-blood. As trains still terminated many miles short in 1839, steamships, despite the hardships of The Hard, had no serious rivals. 'Even with the advantages of rail conveyance as far as Brentwood,' asserted one Victorian traveller, the trip continued thence by road was 'so fatiguing and inconvenient, compared with the facility and rapidity of a down-course by steamers on the Thames, that to expect people will prefer *that* line of communication is absurd!'

Steamer services were not suppressed with the railways' expansion but dovetailed with them to the profit of both. Networks of shipping lines connected resorts right round Britain's coastlines, necessitating the building of proper iron piers, most of which survive as central features, creating an engineering-cum-architectural style as uniform in

Pier, prom, bathing-machines and beach: the ideal combination pictured in Paignton in about 1898.

its way as the Victorian chapel or pub. Even 'seaside' resorts well short of the real sea did roaring trade, as did Gravesend; as late as 1875 it was as famous for shrimp stalls as Leigh-on-Sea was for cockles. At its two piers, built before railway competition, in 1832 and 1843, 1¼ million pleasure-seekers landed in the average season, 250,000 in June alone, when Gregarious Gravesend rivalled Merry Margate. Merry, indeed, were those shrimp-eaters, thanks to the celebrated Halfway House Inn, exactly 13⅛ miles below the Pool, 'much resorted to by passengers who here congratulated themselves on the completion of half their journey'.

Steam boats brought the pier age, as opposed to the age of small jetties and quays, into full operation, when piers originally intended to be functional developed also into the pleasure centres of the resorts served. Journeys of twelve sickly hours shrank to six or seven; yet diehards, as always, mourned the passing of decrepit, comfortless vessels as Jaguar travellers today confess secret affection for long defunct black 1930s Fords. Thus Lamb, as Elia: 'Can I forget thee, thou old Margate hoy . . . ill exchanged for the foppery and freshwater niceness of the modern steam packet?' that sailed 'poisoning the breath of ocean with sulphurous smoke, a great sea Chimera, chimneying and

Everything that could be sold was sold on a pier and its approaches, particularly large exotic shells and trinket boxes trimmed with smaller English shells; this stall was found at Littlehampton, in 1890.

furnacing the deep'. Sentiment looked more fondly than realistically back at those wretched hoys when squalls drove passengers below, 'catering for our comfort with cards, cordials, strong drink and thy more cordial conversation' that made up for the 'not very savoury . . . little cabin'.

Long-distance steam voyaging became common, with 'Grand Yachting Cruises' serving 'Cornwall, Devon, Wilts, Sussex, Kent, Essex, Hants, Surrey [on sea?] and the Isle of Wight'; London to Scotland routes at 'First Cabin, including Steward's fee, 22s; Second Cabin, 16s; Deck — soldiers and sailors only — 10s'; and pure holiday routes. As late as 1937 visitors commonly sailed to Torquay via Plymouth, changing to local steamer or train for the final miles. The awful spectre of unstabilised seasickness deterred few, if contemporary accounts speak true of ships, in Grandma's words, 'black with people'; nor did Disraeli's celebrated anti-ocean tirade, 'I never saw the use of the sea; many a sad heart it has caused, and many a sick stomach it has occasioned; the boldest sailor climbs aboard with a heavy soul, and leaps on land with a light spirit.' Steamers were a way of seaside life, and 'Arrival of the London Boat' became one of Yarmouth's best-selling postcards. They were the royal way to arrive, as well as the Bloggs' automatic choice when bent on Herne Bay winkles, as when the future Edward VII visited Weymouth, to be sung the length of the pier by ranks of children lisping *God Bless the Prince of Wales*; or when George V paced the same boards lined with those childrens' grandchildren, dutifully warbling *God Save the King*, followed

46

'Admission One Penny', a strangely deserted Rhyl pier in 1891.

by retinues of town pomposities. For the Bloggs, the town porters had to suffice, a service highlighted in a Red Guide account of Llandudno.

To and from the station 3d, Pier entrance 4d. The above charges do not include carriage of luggage from the Pier entrance to the Steamers. Certain porters are specially licensed by the Pier Company, and convey baggage from any part of the town to the steamers . . . . Visitors departing by Steamer should be careful to ascertain whether the porter they engage is one of the Pier porters, otherwise they may be disappointed to find that their baggage has been left at the Marine Drive entrance to the Pier instead of being taken directly to the ship.

Today's Majorca tourist whose luggage proves to be still reposing at Gatwick is but yesterday's Liverpudlian discovering that his trunk is still in Llandudno.

The world is all alike, too, in cashing in wherever there are people with purses. Local traders needed little thought to sense potential profit in the celebratory air of any pier's opening day. They created its next phase, an overlapping of function (arrival and departure) with fun; fun that had to be paid for, with pennies fed into slot machines.

Garishness ousted plain announcement-board utility as pier entrances became gaudier allurements to the Bloggs of this world; fairground paintwork by day became by night flarelight, gaslight and, ultimately, all the harsh primary colours of neon that a better-class granny shudderingly termed 'those horrible lights, dear'.

'Admission One Penny' no longer implied mere harbour dues but a penn'orth of fun, followed by a trip by boat, then further amusements on the return walk down the pier. Few resorts saw cause for pride in

47

such an unusual boast as Weymouth made in 1907 that, Channel Island departures apart, 'unlike the piers at most seaside resorts, this is the quietest spot in town.'

Peace was the average visitor's unlikeliest requirement, but for a minority in Bath chairs hired at 1s 6d (7½p) hourly, pushed to the quieter angler-inhabited pierhead ('Bath chair, occupant and attendant 6d' charged Llandudno in about 1919) and there left to breathe ozone and meditate the iniquitous imposition of an additional fourpence for 'Bath chair and attendant only' when his pusher returned to collect him. After all, 'perambulator and attendant' cost only fourpence; and in 1919 that vehicle might contain twins plus young Nellie perched on top; and two further juveniles counted financially as only one gouty colonel. As for those young scallywags in striped blazers, tearing disgracefully around on cycles, who paid pier toll themselves, yet were often allowed to park their pestilential machines free; did not Eastbourne clearly state: 'Cycles can be placed in a stand on the Pier, but as no charge is made for this accommodation, they are there at the owner's risk?'

Much they cared about chair-ridden Colonel Comberleigh-Crane, beyond a passing insolent 'Gaffer!' in legging it towards the penny-in-the-slot machines whose descendants today lure very similar clientele, our electronic horse-racing games and one-armed bandits. 'What The Butler Saw' was the pre-1939 bandit, a four-word synonym for pier; though what the butler saw, in the person of supposedly dirty minded Bert Bloggs, peering through a dark funnel-shaped contraption as his penny dropped, was mild by present standards; a mere glimpse of M'Lady revealing one garter as the peepshow blacked out again. Better entertainment value were similar machines where, for a penny, ghosts crept through bedroom doors, skulls mechanically peered through windows, and a 'skellington' was revealed as a wardrobe door creaked open, though the sleeping lady, of course, stopped decently short of actually jumping out of bed in terror. The penny dropped, and the machinery stopped in time.

What next? The Englishman's instinctive pastime, knocking balls around: skittles, skee-ball, coconut shies, ninepins, shove ha'penny and other sideshows played with water gleaming through the boards underfoot; alternatively, hoop-la stalls, where flinging a thin wooden hoop exactly over a jar from little beyond arm's length looked so easy that one could not imagine oneself not carrying off the prize goldfish in the said bowl, until several pennies had entered the fat stall-holder's pocket. Eastbourne in the 1920s personified piers everywhere in announcing that 'halfway down are ornamental buildings, used as skee-ball and bowling alleys.'

Everything touristically floggable was flogged, from booths flanking the pier entrance short of the actual paybox, as at Weston-super-Mare, to whole clusters of enticements at the far end; there, folk tired by a

48

Tourist souvenirs from three generations: a crested spoon of the 1930s; 1920s china binoculars portraying Brighton but labelled 'Foreign'; and Victorian painted pottery (probably a fish-paste jar) depicting Pegwell Bay.

long plod were psychologically ready to stand, stroll and relax throwing hoops, balls and coins. Some piers also lined the long walk itself at regular intervals with attractive wooden shoplets, rented to local traders, most fascinating of all; at Llandudno, modern tourists can indeed see these same booths and their dainty shell-work stock much as they appeared when that 'handsome iron structure, nearly 800 yards long' was new.

Refreshments ran from sandwiches and beer to more frivolous comestibles such as rock and candy floss. Fruit sold well to small fry, not only to line stomachs but to yield pips for spitting over iron railings onto anglers beneath for or organising spitting contests ('Betcher I can spit farther than *you* can!').

Favourite gifts were wooden trinket boxes covered by elaborate shell work; 'china' dogs of crumbling plaster ('Wotcher expect for tuppence, Ma? Real china?'); Dresden shepherdesses mass produced in Stoke-on Trent (Pa knew that — he chanced to work at the same factory); framed mottoes reading 'Home, Sweet Home'; and innumerable objects inscribed according to selling point 'A Present From . . .'; tiny china binoculars, stamped 'foreign' on the bottom (Brighton souvenirs made in Hong Kong are nothing new), a picture of an undeveloped Brighton no modern eye remembers on each eyepiece;

49

china plates all rosebuds with, in gold, 'A Present from Margate';
spoons with coat-of-arms handles from the Isle of Man to the Isle of
Wight; and crested Blackpool purses and combs. At least as early as
the time of Waterloo, their precursors were available, heavy pottery
souvenirs produced before piers were considered as maritime high
streets; they are typified charmingly by an heirloom of the author's
own family, whereon smocked shrimpers dredge for their catch under
a sparsely inhabited clifftop resort of only one street, where one
building in the fashionable new Regency manner jeers at its neighbours
like a woman at church in a new hat, while vessels built before
Victoria was born ride a painted sea.

That scene is far removed from the great gift shop era fifty or more
years later, when not uncommonly a village quite as large grew up on
the end of an iron pleasure pier, with shops, refreshment houses and
amusements, as at Weston-super-Mare, where these, grouped round a
full-sized clocktower, suggest a landlubber square instead of a steamer
landfall. Always somewhere within such groups was a palmist's tent,
mysteriously curtained, into which many hardly cared to be seen
entering, partly from fear of ridicule ('Ma! Yer surely don't believe
that stuff!'), partly the worse apprehension of being foretold disaster
instead of a dark handsome stranger by she who crooned 'Cross me
hand wi' silver' and plastered the outside of her lair with framed
photographs of royalties and celebrities alleged to have consulted her
advantageously. Nobody, of course, believed it all, but . . . .

Southend pier made a specially convincing island kingdom, not only
being over a mile out at sea but also possessing a full-scale railway
station and trains. Riding that unique railway with seawater lapping
below the sleepers and wooden decking for a permanent way remained
Southend's leading attraction right through to 1976 when the famous
old painted sign 'End of the Longest Pier in the World' overnight took

grimmer meaning, a gateway to fire-blackened wreckage where a hundred years of holiday happiness had stood but yesterday. A fire on the pier, common enough in stiff sea breezes, was a splendid buckshee extra attraction when rebuilding was cheap and provided one was on the right end at the time; in inflated 1976, 'The End of the Pier', smutted with soot, all too probably meant the end of the pier.

Its only serious rival in pier-railwaydom, at Ryde, still performs the double function, commoner before 1939 than today, of genuine ship to shore transport and pleasure tripping. Its story is the whole story of railed travel; horse-drawn tram; electric tram (one of the world's earliest); petrol-driven railcar; puffing steam railway train; finally and uniquely, the only place where discarded London Underground trains run on a seaside pier. Few resorts give us a better insight into the train-steamer-pier-train sequence of Victorian and Edwardian holiday travel, including its rigours of crowds and luggage hauling, than Ryde.

Cameo card showing Great Yarmouth pier; these were all the rage in about 1910.

Baggage and non-queuing humanity, however, belonged to arrival and departure days. Otherwise, piers represented Pleasure with a capital P, FUN in triple capitals and relaxation for rows of deckchair dozers convalescing between shying coconuts and slogging upstairs to marvel at the camera obscura. Even those convalescent interludes were not wholly idle; for every Pa snoozing with a handkerchief over his face there was a mother too busy with children to sleep and an Uncle Sam, ex-Navy, hard at work criticising every yachtsman in sight through the binoculars he had recklessly bought, tempted by an advertisers' boast: 'Finest obtainable for accuracy, clearness of vision and field of view' as binoculars 'complete with leather case and sling' should be at over four hard-earned quid.

Binoculars picked up yachts well enough for Uncle Sam, but the camera obscura reflected for all the family the entire circle of the immediate universe, around, below and behind, within the apparently

51

simple shallow white bowl, at waist height inside a wooden cupola high above pier-pavilion level, around which groups assembled before the attendant shut the door on the expanding queue outside. Claustrophobically the chamber plunged into darkness, except for that magic bowl, several feet across, softly illuminated through a small rooftop hole, from which a convex lens and sloped mirrors reflected down onto the white surface, as if onto a movie screen, images of everything outside, in subdued colour: toylike trains; trams on the parade; people and ships; a band playing; policemen, bathing-machines and bathers. Did not the attendant finally open the door, letting in daylight to destroy the picture and admit another thirty tuppence worths, any child could have lingered for hours, fascinated by an invention reputedly four centuries old, yet also looking another century forward towards colour television.

'Want to see it *again!*' bawled baby Will. Mother, neither made of tuppences nor disposed to endure unlimited roarings, probably whipped from her bag, to quieten him, a cheaper movie projector, her vanity mirror. 'Hold it up, level with your eyes. Now move it right, and look over your shoulder through the mirror. What can you see?' Will would, she hoped, remain silenced until he dropped and broke the mirror, riveted by this simple trick rarely taught modern children, enabling him to watch colour movies in his own hand. Auntie Min caught buying postcards in a mirror was somehow more spellbinding than Auntie Min in person.

Suddenly — one can imagine Will's mirror-twiddling halting — the advertisements MENAGERIE or AQUARIUM enter his sights. Mother's peace is over: 'Want to see the FISH!'

Even the giant garish word FUNFAIR might appear on certain piers, advertising complete fairgrounds over water and under cover. Weston-super-Mare possessed, and still possesses, two separate piers, one a genuine steamer stage with pleasure attachments, the other with few maritime pretences, ending far short of low-tide mark, dedicated purely to amusements; there, in a vast pierhead hall, generations of holidaymakers, even during the Second World War, have enjoyed a full-sized fair complete with big dipper (scenic railway, in earlier parlance), helter skelter tower, terrifying wire cages each containing one passenger, rotating right up and over a bar like circular swings, dodgem cars and roundabouts — everything expected of landlubber fairs. Fair going on pier-plank firma instead of on grass gave very special meaning to that favourite 'Out' game, played while parents rested halfway between promenade and pierhead:

> One, two, three, four, five, six, seven,
> All good children go to Heaven.
> Penny on the water, tuppence on the sea,
> Throop'nce on the roundabout, and OUT goes he.

Postcard humour from the seaside's declining years.

Some resorts offered a less common alternative to pierhead dodgem cars, under or near the pier itself, as did Lowestoft: dodgem boats, where the object of a certain sporty minority was not to dodge but to ram other craft and dislocate their occupants' necks or half drown them, hence the presence of prowling officials' boats keeping order for average families' safety.

'Diving Prohibited' is a common warning on modern piers, but before 1939 the pitting of human necks against water from such heights was not merely allowed but sometimes encouraged, both as a personal version of Russian roulette and as a paid public spectacle.

> And now I'm here,
> From this 'ere pier
> It is my fixed intent,
> To jump, as Mr Levi did,
> From off the Monument,

wrote Barham of *Ingoldsby* fame in his *Misadventures at Margate* in 1830. Jumping for cash was the fixed intent roughly a century later, of such characters as the much publicised Lady Diver of neighbouring Herne Bay, drawing crowds twice daily to watch her daring feats of balletic-athletic grace from a diving board projecting, like a pirate ship's infamous plank, from the seaward side of the projecting railings. Herne Bay without the Lady Diver was for juniors like Margate without a donkey ride.

Show-off young fellows in black hired drawers regularly drew spectators, plunging from pierheads into deepest water; but, as Eastbourne emphasised at the same period, such feats were only masculine, except when booked professionally like female circus stunts: 'There is . . . a dressing room for bathers, gentlemen only' ran the regulations, at a cost of '6d, season ticket 9s'. Anyone intending to extract nine shillings' worth of diving, when that amount approximated to a modern fiver, needed to live locally and emulate a sealion many times a week.

Divers, amateur or professional, were alike the bane of legions of fishermen ensconced on staging under the main pier, imitating motionless blocks of cast iron; divers whose floundering always drove off the monster catch of a lifetime split seconds before actually biting, robbing them of an answer to the often quoted old fisherman's prayer:

> God grant that I should catch a fish
> So big, that even I,
> When telling of it afterwards.
> May have no need to lie.

So was launching the lifeboat a nuisance to dedicated anglers, but to 99.9 per cent of any pier's patronage it was an entertainment always to be hoped for. Margate lifeboat sliding down its slipway in fountains of spray to an enormous splash was a real holiday highlight; chance alone surely did not dictate that one little May, scrawling in a childish hand in 1918, 'We are having such a fine time, wish you were here', chose

Dodgem boats, less common than dodgem cars, a popular diversion usually installed beside or under the pier.

a spectacular sepia postcard showing the said lifeboat being launched to express the ecstasy of Margate when holidays were brief and six-pennorth of excitement had to be crammed into every penny hour.

> If all the seas were one sea, what a great sea that would be;
> If all the trees were one tree, what a great tree that would be;
> And if that tree fell into the sea,
> What a mighty splash there would be!

Every child old enough to learn nursery rhymes knew that versified splash of splashes. Watching the lifeboat made it come true, seen from the pier after a perfect morning of swings, roundabouts, camera obscura and menageries, before going back to second helpings at the Misses Thomkins' Seaview Select Boarding Establishment, was very heaven when one old penny bought as much pleasure on the pier as a decimalised pound today.

5. *Smile Please*

What have the father of the railways, cotton-mill workers, and the initiator of an Act of Parliament in common? Between them, they turned the select Georgian esplanade or promenade into the prom-prom-prom-tiddly-om-pom-pom, taken over from sedately-pacing carriage-class gentry by workers released for the first time by legislation at certain times during summer for uncerebral, rowdily happy enjoyment of life, in whose face Society fled back to inland spas or to certain resorts destined to retain Eton accents when all around were succumbing to broad Lancashire or Cockney cockiness.

Promenades, like piers, thus underwent three distinct phases: the elegant esplanade era; a transitional Seafront season; and the final uninhibited prom period.

Phase one originated in wealth and royalty, Society following in better-bred fashion the crowds of local gapers dogging George III's steps along Weymouth esplanade, ruthlessly leading a train of reluctant princesses and ladies, at the allegedly healthy but ungodly morning hour of six. If early promenading was correct for a king, every pretender to social standing automatically did likewise and pretended to enjoy it.

Without railways, only wealth could thus follow wealth to the bathing-machines. Resorts more closely resembled spas than maritime funfairs, gracious retreats where parents were addressed as Mama and Papa and kept at least one nannie for Miss Cicely, Miss Nina and Master Edward, all too ponderously packaged in ribbons and velvets to enjoy anything more seasidey on the promenade than bowling sedate hoops. Returning the compliment of formality even on holiday, they spoke always of the Grand or Marine Parade, Upper Drive, Undercliff or Esplanade in full; shortening a promenade into so vulgar a diminutive as prom was unladylike, indeed unthinkable.

Social intercourse, as at the Spas, often revolved round a Master of Ceremonies. Eld, Brighton's final M.C. before trains destroyed its Regency exclusivity for ever, cultivated the same air of owning Brighton, including old ocean himself, as Beau Nash once did in imposing his Rules of Bath; 'A gentleman attired in point-device, walking down the Parade, like Agag, ''delicately'',' (as one who knew him wrote) 'he

The old seaside postcard humour fell well short of vulgarity. This card, posted during the First World War, was inscribed, 'Well, old son, Ta-ta, and pile up the munitions.'

55

SEASIDE SPORTS.

A SUGGESTION FOR A WET DAY. BATH-CHAIR RACE ALONG THE DESERTED PARADE. THE LAST PAST THE POST PAYS FOR ALL CHAIRS.

Punch jazzes up the invalid population on a wet promenade in 1898.

pointed out his toes like a dancing master, but carried his head like a potentate.' From the Parade, Eld could be observed continuing onto the pier.

There I observed him look first over the right side and then over to the left, with an expression of serene satisfaction spreading over his countenance which said, as plainly as if he had spoken it to the sea aloud: 'That is right; you are low tide at present; but never mind, in a couple of hours I shall make you high tide again.'

Invalids — genuine as well as *malades imaginaires* — formed half Brighton's population in the 1840s, socially a million centuries away but in reality separated by only thirty years from the horrors of Bank Holidays, when Thackeray observed 'the cabs, the flys, the shandry-dans, the sedan chairs, with poor invalids inside; the old maids, the dowagers' chariots, out of which you see countenances scarcely less deathlike'. Even youth was not yet bucket-and-spade youth, in both emotions and behaviour as tightly reined as the 'young ladies from the equestrian schools, by whose side the riding masters cantered confidently', and hopelessly hopefully.

Infant Miss Nina's promenade was no childish stumble on foot, interspersed by grizzles and chortles, but a sedate perambulation in an elaborate wicker-work pushchair whose charm posterity has almost forgotten — the mail-cart not made for delivering mail but for transporting children, sturdy, lowslung, intricately woven yet lightweight, whose like we must journey some 1500 miles to Madeira to see for ourselves today. Expensive twin mail-carts, portrayed by appropriately expensive local studios, are today's photographic rarities, preserving both this intricate form of baby carriage, which survived little beyond the turn of the present century, and the unchildlike childhoods of those whose parents considered getting clothes grubby, like using the word prom instead of Marine Parade, somewhat vulgar.

When invalids sought the sea for health, instead of the healthy seeking it for pleasure, bath chairs and cabs were also familiar sights. Fresh air, however, was not everyone's notion of beneficial breathing material, even if mobile enough for gentle exercise. Thus in 1840 we read of Society at Torquay, miserably huddled against the slightest suggestion

56

of mist: 'The Frying Pan Walk along the Strand [is] filled in general with respirator-bearing people, who look like muzzled ghosts and are ugly enough to frighten younger people to death.' The unmuzzled could hardly have been more inspiring to anyone under a respectable sixty: on one average day upon the Frying Pan Walk were observed '82 spinsters, 19 medicals, 12 divines, and . . . 2 attorneys', without either an eligible young man or even a child of high spirits anywhere in sight.

The very word Promenade in fact brought to mind sedate, unholiday-fied holiday-makers on the move, as much as a paved walk on the seafront itself, seeing and being seen by acceptable people, acknowledging their greater or lesser rank with the appropriate depth of a bow or nod.

Nor was promenading assumed to apply only at sea level. Afternoon Promenade, an important Scarborough formality, meant clifftop strolls across the spectacular chasm bridge between town and New Spa buildings, at the opening of which in 1827 'a bold charioteer with four well trained steeds in hand, undertook . . . to drive a coach over it amid the acclamations of the myriads who covered the adjoining buildings and surrounding hills, which on that eventful day for Scarborough were swarming with human faces.' A great event was the acquisition of any resort's chief amenity, a promenade.

Scarborough demonstrated the overlapping of the seaside and the spa ages, chancing also to be a spa in its own right, as Society migrated from Bath's winter season to a socially obligatory summer sojourn at the coast, transferring there the same artificialities, insincerities and graces practised before the same companions; meeting, greeting and departing with the same consciousness of position and breeding, like formal human puppets. 'The bearing of many of these visitors bespoke the rank in life to which they appertained,' enthused one who came, saw and was suitably impressed in 1839; 'Lady R____, relict of the opulent Yorkshire baronet . . . Colonel M____ and his lovely family, nearly all allied in blood to a recently deceased earl; Sir L.O____; the Rev. Dr F____', plus a goodly gathering of countesses, lords, honourables and others of 'superior class'.

Promenading at Scarborough varied little from promenading at Cheltenham; the sea was but an expanse to be contemplated with sober appreciation, remembering last Sunday's sermon on nature's infinity and man's mortality, attended among refined company, rather than waters for plunging into with with uninhibited whoops. As another idealist penned of infant Aldeburgh in 1813, the place could not 'fail to delight the lover of nature' with its 'magnificent terrace on the summit of the hill behind the town, commanding a view that embraces many features, both of the sublime and beautiful'. That cheery penny amusements could ever replace sublimity and beauty as primary coastal requirements was unimaginable.

57

On the 'Prom-prom-prom-tiddly-om-pom-pom' at Worthing immediately after the end of the Great War.

Railways, workers' days off, Bank Holidays and Wakes Weeks, however, wrought that very change, within a few breathless decades, precipitating the leisured esplanade era into the seafront stage or prom period according to resort and company. Seasides slotted themselves almost automatically into categories, according to which type of holiday-maker they attracted. They in turn brought more of like mind, consolidating a permanent trend.

Some, like Torquay, continued exuding such a tangible air of 'class' that workers, freed by railways to explore their own country and given days off and later full weeks in which to do so, instinctively shunned them. Torquay would always be basically Torquay, periodically invaded by Bank Holiday trippers but quickly regaining its year-round Grand Hotel image with a sigh of relief on their departure. Other resorts, conversely, changed completely, like Regency Brighton, too near London to escape a tripper take-over; society fled as the first jam-packed trains gasped into its new station to blaring welcoming brass bands, pouring out Londoners dedicated to turning its sedate Seafront into a happy, slightly rapscallionly and abbreviated Front, smelling of pies and fried fish. Most resorts, however, merely expanded their earlier reputations; Margate, described in the eighteenth century as 'Bartholomew Fair by the seaside' (not exactly a compliment), continued under the sobriquet Merry Margate, abandoning its brief period of half-hearted pretence as a goal for the 'cit' who went 'haughtily bending his head backwards as though in dread of being thought to have contracted a sneaking stoop behind a counter' to acknowledge that most of its arrivals *did* spend their lives behind counters or workbenches, accordingly making its main attraction an unsophisticated noisy, cheerful, booth-lined Prom.

58

Sea-front fashions at
Gorleston in 1918.

Blackpool likewise continued from childhood into adulthood without change. Blackpool of the gipsy beach amusements would never be anything but a bigger and bigger pleasure beach, whose enticements expanded hundredsfold with the advent of a Tower, three piers and a Prom intended to out-prom all other Proms and Golden Miles, until it could call itself the Pleasure Capital of Europe. Even in 1840 Blackpool boasted its South Pier, whilst Southend's single pier was but a recurring item on a reluctant council's agenda, plus a new esplanade, according to an impressed 1840 topographer: 'Between the extreme north end of the village and the recently erected South Pier, a terrace nearly opposite Nixon's [Hotel] has been established, which serves as a marine promenade to pedestrians as well as the equestrians returning from the sands.' The main clientele, too, was already established. 'The manufacturing inhabitants of Lancashire supply most of the company at Blackpool; it is rarely that the superior classes of Preston come hither', congregating instead on 'the less primitive shores of Brighthelm-stone'. Differences became noticeable between resorts geographically close but otherwise strangely contrasted; residents of St Anne's would always regard themselves as superior and pronounce their habitation with subtle accentuation of the 'Saint' (in full, audibly capitalised); as modest Clevedon of the graceful iron-lacework pier would always deport itself peaceably whilst Weston-super-Mare rejoiced in unbuttoned fun, donkey rides, candy floss and conjurors. At Clevedon, Mama and Papa rarely fell below the nomenclature Mother and Father; their children, sensibly attired in black-buttoned boots and straw or sailor hats, bore respectable names like Ellen, Irene and Dorothy, shortened at worst into Nellie, Renie and Dolly, but never truncated into Nell, Reen and Dot; diminutives, considered

Trams and horse-drawn
wagons on Marine Parade,
Yarmouth, in about 1918.

common, belonged to noisier Weston, mispronounced Wessun by Bristol
artisans content to be Ma and Pa and round up their broods with calls
of 'Bert! Gert! Ern!', keeping up with the Jones's by trundling baby
Ed in a cheap mail-cart or its cheaper and uglier successor, a big black
perambulator, acquired on hire-purchase at a shilling a week and still
only half paid-off when another baby appeared, reduced verbally to
pram as surely as the promenade along which it bowled with squeaking
axles was shortened to Prom.

Bristolians thus migrated to Weston, first on half-days, then whole
days, soon on short real holidays, as Londoners swarmed into 'Sarfend-
on-Mud' to consume cockles or East Anglians descended on Clacton's
amusements, throughout the summer. But mass exodus of entire
townships together, into only one or two resorts, during the same few
weeks, was a phenomenon peculiar to the north. The famous Wakes
Weeks, more than anything else, made Blackpool synonymous with
hearty, unpretentious, penny-in-the-slot, happy family fun.

Wakes originated centuries before Blackpool was anything but a dour,
reed-fringed black pool by a bleakly deserted shore, as deeply pious watch-
nights on the dedication feasts of churches. The truly faithful kept
a-wake and a-praying till dawn, after which the whole village rejoiced in
the name of its patron saint in the church square. As secular elements
overtook ecclesiastical aspects the word wake became attached not to
the church vigil but to the following merry-making day, a beanfeast
anticipated with excitement for weeks in advance. Booths and stalls
crammed the square; gipsies and mendicants arrived, hawking wares,
pies, ribbons and sweetmeats; at Ely, cheap trinkets sold under the
excuse of Etheldreda or Audrey, the local patroness, were shouted

abroad as 'St. Audries!' or 'S'nt 'awdries, originating our term for all glittering but cheap objects — tawdry; farmers' wives rode in with cheeses for sale and bursting with bottled-up gossip. There were innumerable reunions between parents, married daughters and grand-children, to whom ten miles by jostling carrier's cart was the average boundary of travel. As early as the twelfth century, wakes as holy days were degenerating into public holidays, when country-folk grasped hungrily at every excuse for fun, knowing the next fair was a long way ahead — exactly as Bolton and Manchester cotton millers grasped the Wakes fun of Blackpool with both calloused hands seven hundred years later, knowing that their release from mills and benches was likewise precious and brief.

England as a whole replaced the word wake by simple holiday except up north. There, wake still spelled a beano, whose only surviving connection with the church was concern for the mood of one particular saint, Swithin, traditional prophet of rain. Persistent bad weather, whether St Swithin's fault or not, during those vital weeks precipitated the final break with church tradition, notably for Bolton whose holidays fell at fickle Whitsuntide, with a briefer August weekend. Textile workers' agitations succeeded in transferring the main breaks, Wakes Weeks (Manchester) and Holiday Weeks (Bolton), to more reliable June and July, each individual mill town following in fixing its own Wakes dates. Over a hundred towns' holiday dates are still officially classified today and announced publicly by Manchester Royal Exchange; moves to abandon Wakes custom, entire towns closing down while their populations migrate to stereotyped seasides, have met little favour. So deeply engrained is tradition as to produce the reaction: 'Don't tamper with the holiday system; it's more convenient, and everyone knows exactly where they stand.' Similarly, attempts to publicise Bolton's preference for the title Holiday Weeks instead of Wakes Weeks finds no favour on hidebound Blackpool landladies' tongues.

In 1871 the Bank Holidays Act introduced by a Liberal with working mens' welfare at heart, Sir John Lubbock, Principal of the London Working Mens' College, rammed the final nail into the coffin of other resorts' diminishing selectness, at least during August. Lanca-shire's second, shorter Wakes, by adopting the same weekend, finalised the image of annual universal jollity, happily vulgar and uninhibited, which turned the smallest resort into a temporary rail- or steamer-borne Bedlam. Bank Holidays made the word Prom synonymous with seaside pleasure for Everyman.

Bank Holidays even today are not ideal times for transcendental meditation; but thanks to greater freedom in choosing holiday dates and our *blasé* insistence on comparing Torquay disparagingly with Torremolinos, the Exeter by-pass at its worst appears tranquil against August almost exactly a century ago, when one day off was as treasured as a fortnight is now. The entire population moved collectively

coastwards, riverwards or parkwards. Shops shut up and died, trade
ceased, making eerily deserted streets disconsolate places for those too
poor to afford a train fare to Margate nor able to find one blade of grass
in a local park free to receive another reclining posterior. Thus
lamented a wanderer in his strangely stilled home town, ironically left
dejected by the very Act designed to create pleasure:

> The country crammed — the seaside jammed —
> The trains a crush — the River a rush —
> Oh, is it not a JOLLY day?
> All shops shut — the Streets all smut —
> No room in the Park for a poor Bank clerk —
> Not a Bank, but a BLANK Holiday!

Thenceforth, for all but a few exceptions such as he, Bank Holiday
on the seething crowded Prom crowned summer, with queues spilling
out of station booking-halls halfway up suburban high streets, to buy
five-bob returns to Margate and travel in conditions even a modern
rush-hour commuter would find almost intolerable; jam-packed,
standing, deafened by squalling babies and hissing steam, arriving with
painful smuts in the eyes from engines belching in tunnels, but at the
sea. That was all that mattered into the 1920s and 1930s, heyday of
the Bank Holiday spirit.

August Bank Holiday, 1926, was the record-breaking climax.
Southend, an excellent mirror of the national trend, was 'swamped by a
tidal wave of visitors', jamming every hotel. Still thousands poured in
by river and rail, turning the six-mile long Prom into one vast
dormitory. Quite ten thousand sleepers snored that night outdoors on
the Prom, beach and cliffs, each family setting up a sentry to preserve
its precious pitch against ever more invaders and another to tend its
camp fire. Thousands of bright flickering flames made a fairyland of
sparks, until an unromantic police force ordered their extinction. In
warm darkness, bathers splashed in a midnight high tide, knowing that
the foreshore would revert to less sparkling Sarfend-on-Mud seven
hours afterwards, their shouts unheard by snoozers lucky enough to
occupy benches in Promenade shelters, breakwaters or upturned boats.
A few even found hard but flat beds — the counters of closed winkle
and cockle stalls. Another half thousand, by courtesy of a thoughtful
cinema proprietor, woke refreshed to tomorrow's beano from softer
beds, having been allowed to pass that night in the stalls of his dimly-lit
theatre. Possibly 1926 was the only year in which uninhibited Southend
could be accused of literally going to sleep for part of a Bank Holiday;
for one national newspaper reported the incredible line of outdoor
snoozers stretched six full miles, all the way to distant Shoeburyness. If
that was the night, what would the day bring?

For many, it brought only a longing for a good sleep to get over a
bad sleep, by waking early enough to collar a deckchair, breathing a
thankful prayer to whoever invented that comfortable canvas contraption,
unaware that the deckchair, most essential item of all Prom furniture,

TO BRIGHTEN THE LITTLE ONES' HOLIDAYS.

THE PATENT DONKEY ACCELERATOR.

A whimsical *Punch* automaton gets out the whip in 1908 to liven up the sedater type of seaside.

reputedly originated just across the water by steamer from Southend pier, at equally happy and Bank Holidayfied Merry Margate.

Margate and Southend were twin meccas for East Londoners when Father Thames' tideway was as thick with churning paddle-steamers as the permanent way outside Waterloo is today with trains, mostly crossing to Margate after swapping a thousand trippers at Southend for another thousand bound for Kent. There they deposited a cross-section of London artisanry: publicans and street singers; buskers and brick-makers; grocers, carpenters and owners of small private joineries, few rejoicing in more high-falutin' surnames than Smith and Jones, in those reflecting their forefathers' occupations (Tanner, Cooper, Baker) or in those short and simple, like Atkins.

Edwin Atkins of Bethnal Green was more loaded that the Bakers and Coopers when, with his family, he staggered onto Margate Prom one day in 1898, lumbered in addition to coats and baggage with, of all things, six chairs made in his own works, of canvas nailed onto wooden frames: but onlookers' titters turned to envy when the Atkinses settled comfortably into their own beach chairs, wherever they chose, instead of squatting on sand. Presumably because landladies objected to imported furniture in addition to luggage, Atkins left them in a Margate boatman's care .

Every facility on a typical busy promenade at Blackpool: trams, buses, souvenir stalls, cafes and crowds, crowds and more crowds.

His holiday paid handsomely for itself. Instead of saying no to those begging to borrow a chair, Father said yes — at a small fee — and took the gamble of ordering despatch of a hundred from London, persuading the boatman to become a concessionaire on commission. If the hundred failed to earn their keep in a week, the boatman would pay nothing. Instead he ordered a second hundred. Margate Prom and beach boasted what was probably Britain's earliest line of deckchairs, despite counter-claims from other resorts.

Prom architecture and furnishing between then and about 1910 took such a distinctive air that one glance differentiated its principal features from any ordinary carriageway: public seats, shared but free of charge; deckchairs; fancy iron lamp-brackets, noticeably complementing the Royal Pavilion at Brighton's neighbour, Worthing; knobbled iron railings; ornate ironwork shelters and kiosks; bandstands and pavilions; and commemorative clock towers. These were the so-called Victorian and Edwardian 'monstrosities' deprecated in the 1950s which we now, rightly, realise are a heritage; who, barely twenty years ago, dreamed that the charming Bexhill shelter nicknamed Queen Victoria's Hatbox would in 1976 be listed as of outstanding historical or architectural interest?

Architectural heritages were of scant concern to generations of holiday-makers who therein read newspapers, nursed snapping Pekes, wiped infants' noses and munched fish and chips; least of all to those who spooned, canoodled, courted, cuddled or went all-doolally, according to the language of their days; nor did they display delight when electricity replaced softer seafront gaslight, piercing intimate corners of the appropriately named Cosies walk of Gorleston or the formerly dim shelters of Llandudno.

Llandudno's inter-war boast was to no canoodler's taste: 'The town is very progressive . . . . The Promenade and shelters are illuminated at night by electric light, and are so bright that visitors take their books and evening paper to read while listening to the band.' Minehead was worse, with firebells added to disturb lovers' concentration. ('The town is lighted by gas and electricity, and has an efficient voluntary fire brigade with a motor fire engine.') As for Blackpool and Southend: having acquired the taste of electricity, like children experimenting with new toys, there was no holding them, until Prom illuminations no longer involved mere public safety but became in their own right these resorts' greatest and most profitable public spectacles. Ever bigger, they stretched for several dazzling night miles, lengthening the season and expanding profits into autumn. Lamps festooned round posts, in colour instead of white, were but a step from swathes of lights across the Prom. Then came light on the move, transforming common trams and buses into Mississippi showboats, Cinderella coaches and ocean liners; plus static set-pieces of mechanical birds fighting for electrically-wriggling worms, Popeye, and Mickey Mouse. Ultimately, the sky itself was not immune from man's hand on the light switch, as searchlights stabbed aloft over Blackpool Tower.

A Tower: every resort should have one. That was the theme of hopeful potential Blackpools, mostly doomed never to materialise. There could be only one genuine Blackpool Tower, soaring 500 feet above leisure nests of ballrooms, theatres, circus rings and restaurants; so famous that, across the Atlantic, it was a natural choice of American postcard publishers comparing the now defunct Singer Skyscraper with world landmarks. Great Yarmouth tried, with a curious rounded skeletal Tower, resembling the girder skeleton of a Crystal Palace tower unclothed by glass, topped by a massive Union Jack; but New Brighton gave up at a vast fortress-like bottom-stage stump, left forlornly incomplete for decades afterwards by a sometimes dismal shore, without power to magnetise the hoped-for multitudes whom instinct drove to bigger seasides in company with thousands of like mind, where bandstands advertised nothing more 'hedificated' than *We Do Love to be beside the Seaside*, between soothing *Rose Marie* selections and innocent ballads of the *Pale Hands I Loved* variety. 'Good Stuff', meaning music above Ma's and Pa's heads, was reserved for places such as Bournemouth; though even there, none who heard young Dan Godfrey's band in mock-military pillboxes give their first concert one nineteenth-century Bank Holiday could possibly have dreamed that under Godfrey's cap swam dreams of classical music for the masses or that his little band was the seed of the Bournemouth Symphony Orchestra, famous today for performing standards recognised as far away as Moscow. True, certain other resorts built themselves theatres called opera houses; but who expected, or wanted, to find *Die Meistersinger* on their bills?

Organ-grinders were more to Pa's taste, or gramophones with long horns mounted on old babies' prams, trundled along side-streets lined with boarding-houses, just off the main Prom, grinding out popular music-hall ditties while a pathetic monkey in scarlet jacket on top held out trained paws for pennies. They existed long before Bank Holidays, for in about 1800 we can read of a street organ 'with gold organ pipes in front', piano organs, barrel organs wound by a cumbersome handle, playing everything from light opera to sobbing love songs and *The Ratcatcher's Daughter*, and 'the one with figure dolls in front' round which legions of children gathered to listen to the dolls' hypnotic tap-tap of wooden feet and chant:

> Dancing Dolly had no sense;
> Bought a fiddle for eighteen pence;
> The only tune that she could play
> Was 'Over the Hills and Far Away'.

The promenade and beach at Great Yarmouth, quieter than Blackpool, yet with every amenity.

Street vendors were regular features of seaside towns as much as cities well into the present century; watching the cats' meat man of Burnham-on-Sea on his rounds of boarding-houses (each supporting one moggie on the pay-roll as mouser and larder guardian), followed by assorted hopeful felines with tails expectantly in the air, was as entertaining for holiday children as it was for the locals.

So was the sport of chanting 'Yah!' barely behind the backs of crusty colonels in Bath chairs. Llandudno expected sufficient droves of arthritics to hire out Bath chairs as freely as deckchairs and advertised that: 'For the convenience of invalids, and others who desire to regulate the amount of their daily exercise, the Promenade has been marked off into quarter-mile distances,' like the boat deck of the great liners that were a rich colonel's other natural habitat. Long after the Armistice, Eastbourne acknowledged the commercial profitability of hiring Bath chairs, though inflation, another scourge we wrongly assume to be purely modern, had by then rocketed charges to '2s an hour; 3s for 1½ hours; 6d each subsequent ½ hour'.

Sunday-go-to-Meeting traditions, again, continued into George V's reign, when it was said of Llandudno: 'Church Parade along this magnificent stretch at the height of the Season is a sight to be remembered' — not for entirely Christian reasons but for the spectacle of everyone from ladies to costers' wives in their Sunday best, expensively simple of cut or ostentatiously frilled and feathered according to birthright, pacing the Prom to and from church or chapel at half the hectic speed of Saturday, sparing thought for the ubiquitous sandwich-men saddled back and front with huge daubed bills reading REPENT! THE END OF THE WORLD IS NIGH! after sitting through hour-long sermons with the same un-holidayfied theme.

Thankfully, tomorrow would be Monday and listening to cinema organs or taking donkey rides no longer sinful. Nor would disturbing others' peace seem a sin, in the eyes of certain groups as hooked on portable gramophones as their descendants are on transistor radios; thoughtless folk who were cursed as far back as the classic *Three Men in a Boat* and were still being cursed in 1922 with the advent of the advertiser's suggestion that one make that year 'A RECORD Holiday' with their 'Portable Gramophone, playing the Longest 12-inch Record with unvarying speed at one winding . . . the Finest in the World with Solid Walnut Case, French Polished, plus Seven Discs'. Luckily, not everyone could as yet afford its princely price, £3 upwards.

But everyone could afford sweets and snacks, whose wrappings were scattered upon the good ground of Prom and cliffs quite as prolifically as they are today; every student of social history can only repeat *ad infinitum* that nothing about humanity is new, including litter louts. So bad was the problem between the two wars as to prompt a Royal appeal: 'The King has asked people not to leave rubbish and debris about; public meetings have been held to make the same appeal,' but

the effect was only too predictable. 'Still the litter-leaver makes the
beauty spots he visits unsightly,' complained Torquay, whilst Minehead
reciprocated in verse to no better effect:

> Good friends, who to this spot repair,
> Rest and be thankful; but forbear
> With sordid scraps the ground to strew —
> Others rest here, as well as you!

Asked to nominate seasidedom's prime curses, most would include
uproarious crowds, litter bugs and, later, gramophiles and radiophiles;
but asked to think of something universally pleasing, one particular
thing would surely stand out: the camera, built to preserve the
happiest moments of one week for the other fifty-one of the year.
Those who made, used and serviced them professionally would probably
also have named photography as the greatest money-spinner on the
Prom.

Photo booths were magnets for everyone whose greatest thrill was
seeing his own name in print or his own likeness on film; everyone
from a young lord posing against velvet drapes at Torquay to a
dustman grinning inanely beside his son in striped pants and straw
boater, the latter acquired from the lord's dustbin by the accepted
process of totting (the extraction of saleable cast-offs as perks of the
trade).

Before the Great Exhibition reared its first Crystal Palatial girders,
street photographers operated alongside fruit barrows and piemen.
'Within the last few years photographic portraits have gradually been
diminishing in price, until at the present time they have become a
regular article of street commerce,' wrote one who witnessed both the
Crystal Palace age and the first seaside excursion trains. Sixpenny
portraits from canvas booths came, not on film, but 'a little square

piece of glass . . . scarcely larger than a visiting card' processed and mounted by a pimpled youth behind a dividing curtain into finished jobs that are now historic rarities. As fortune tellers plastered tents with tributes, photographers hung higgledy-piggledy selections of their work outside, 'as irregularly as if a bill-sticker had placed them there', standing beside their little empires bawling 'Hi! Hi! Hi! Walk up! 'Ave yer pick-cher took! Framed and glass complete, only a Tanner!' Quality varied according to the owner's skill, artistic sense, or lack of it, and props. A professional's sepia of a young couple in cameo has a charm few modern studios can excell, but a Prom casher-in's effort at a formal pose with props inspires in posterity only chuckles, showing one's Granny as very young, very self-consciously middle-class, in a contrived anyone-for-tennis pose, clutching a borrowed racquet full of unmended holes, never having hit a ball in all her real life. Later, earthy humour replaced Granny and her prop-racquet, with Ma and Pa Bloggs poking their grinning heads through holes in painted backcloths to become, on film, pirates, nudes, the Fat Boy of Peckham, sport or cinema idols, elephants, or bathing belles of anatomically impossible but satisfyingly ample construction.

To amateur photography posterity owes a more natural record of seaside life after about 1870, though no concern for posterity motivated the finger on the trigger at the time, only remembrance of today until next holiday.

Stereoscopic pair of snapshots taken at Burnham-on-Sea in 1901.

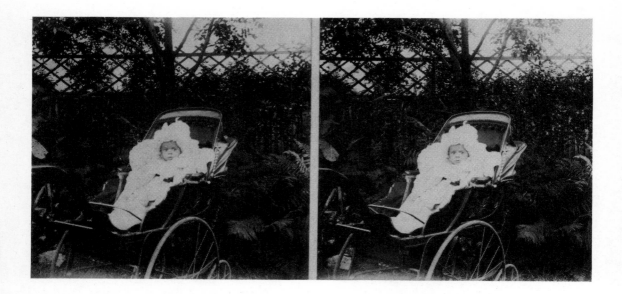

Baby in his heavy black pram: a stereoscopic picture from about 1900.

Once costs fell into Everyman's range, many hotels added in advertisements the blandishment, unheard of now, 'darkroom for photography'. There Uncle Bert might happily go to earth with his Photography Simplified kit or 'Vest Pocket Studio Set', muttering under his breath with prophetically Churchillian ring, 'Some Vest! Some Pocket!' The equipment alleged to fit into the said pocket included one folding bellows camera, developing tank and 'all requisites to make the finished pictures of $2\frac{1}{2} \times 1\frac{3}{8}$ inches', in all, not less than about fifteen tubes, boxes and containers, costing well over fifteen bob down, not to mention several shillings monthly on the never-never.

Infinitely more reliable were the services of the professional camera shops which sprung up in every seafront well before 1918. Why waste so much time, and risk ruining Aunt Fanny's carefully posed profile, when such men as this, of Southwold, promised infallibly: 'Photography is my Business, not a Sideline, and Amateur work is my speciality?' Rollfilm of six shots cost 6d, other film sizes 9d, enlargements 1s each. Quality was sometimes poor, fading in albums to shades of watered-down mud by now; but the best developing services gave results which remain printable, sixty years onwards.

With luck, Uncle's snapshotting could have paid for his holiday, when nationwide competitions were sponsored by such companies as the French-based Pathé, afterwards associated mainly with cinema, who in the 1920s proclaimed that 'TWO persons won NINE prizes in the Brighton Corporation Competition last summer, 1926 . . . . The total value of their prizes was £89'. Nearly £90 covered a whole family's holiday, when a 'five-pound-a-week man' was considered a splendid catch for a daughter. Humour, rather than pretty-pretty entries, was an almost certain winner; father and prospective son-in-law fooling like two Indian braves, peering over a few grass blades, in bowler or trilby hats, shot with an old box Brownie, stood as good a chance — or better — as any characterless stiffly posing family groups.

Prom and beach photography from the start had its gimmicks, notably something few modern snapshotters have ever seen in use, an instrument of astonishing realism, the stereoscope, needing but an uncomplicated wooden viewer for operation. Binocular fashion, pictures in almost identical pairs, mounted on stiff board, were focused to an individual's sight by sliding the wire holder in which they slotted nearer or further from the eye. Once focused, the merged effect of the mounted pair was uncanny; Auntie, Uncle and six other people in the back garden of their diggings each sprang into stereo relief and perspective; every leaf of the runner beans was identifiably in front of or behind each other leaf; Baby in his heavy black pram stood starkly out from his background hedge, every frill of his elaborate lace headgear and pillow distinct, fold from fold; his feet appeared six inches further from the camera than his pram handle, as they were. Present science produces splendid colour slide results and viewers but nothing comparable with the realistic perspective of a stereoscope and pairs, handed down in a family from 1900 or earlier. Nor was it confined to personal snapshotting with a difference. As nowadays we can buy professional slides of Weymouth or Bournemouth to supplement our own, so Granny back in 1900 bought additional stereoscope pairs, ready mounted, in sets: warships, trains or nature study, wherein vipers crawled almost too realistically from foliage and plovers sat on naturalistic nests.

Not quite dead like the stereoscope, but nowadays uncommon, is the once ubiquitous silhouette artist, whose booth and table trapped hundreds at pier and sun-deck entrances. His art dated back at least to the 1850s when it was recorded that any street buyer could thereby acquire 'a tolerably correct profile of himself in black paper, mounted upon a white card' from a 'profilist or silhouette artist'. His technique had changed scarcely a whit in 1939 on the brink of worldwide upheaval, when it was still customary for Grandpa to have his profile cut, posing to throw a shadow around which the artist rapidly drew, whilst Granny and the children waited their turn in open-mouthed admiration. A good profile could preserve for all time an extraordinarily speaking likeness and suggestion of that elusive thing called character.

All good things come to an end, Granny and Grandpa reminded a tearful brood, forced to pack up buckets and spades on Saturday and return to town, though at least some of those good things were preserved fact instead of intangible memory, caught on film and scraps

Simple properties were every promenade photographer's stock in trade: this customer posed with a tennis racquet full of holes and the awkward grip of a girl who has never played tennis.

of profilists' cardboard. They were probably unaware that Shakespeare said the same thing 350 years before; nor would any child dreading return to school have believed them if they *had* quoted the Bard's immortal couplet:

> If all the year were playing holidays,
> To sport would be as tedious as to work.

'Playing holidays' in about 1910.

6. Donkey Serenade

Scotsman's kilt humour on the beach.

'The *idea* of seeing THE SEA! Of being near it — watching its changes by sunrise, sunset, moonlight and noonday — in calm — perhaps — in storm — fills and satisfies my mind,' rhapsodised Charlotte Brontë in 1839, overawed by the prospect of setting eyes upon sands and waves for the first time in her life, translated to Bridlington at a more staggering pace than man had yet known by a sooty magic carpet, wafted not through perfumed air but on iron rails. Bridlington's strand so moved Charlotte that she burst into tears and continued 'very quiet and subdued for the remainder of the day'. Only some of the people already in residence jarred her sensitivity; those stiff spa-orientated puppets, rigidly bound to doing the done thing in the done company instead of openly enjoying life, whose ritual evening pier constitutional she found 'the greatest absurdity'.

Looking down onto the beach itself, however, Charlotte saw the more relaxed Bridlington of children, not far removed from children on the beach today: making sandcastles and shrimping, taking donkey rides and paddling. For a tiny infant, showing both legs bare to the knees was not entirely taboo, so long as her little face was swathed in ruched bonnets and her main anatomy in stiff restrictive folkweave skirts, though many summers would pass before any girl over fourteen could question Grandmama's insistence that the human frame above ankle level was 'not quite nice' and that looking healthily tanned was only for hussies or milkmaids. Half a century onwards from Charlotte Brontë's Bridlington, the south coast continued advertising lack of a tan as a holiday aim: 'Weymouth has one advantage over other . . . resorts; as the beach faces east, there is never a glare off the water from the sun; with the seats on the Esplanade facing seawards, visitors have the convenience and comfort of the sun behind them, and not in their faces.'

In adults' eyes, beaches, as Victoria settled herself onto the throne, were for ladylike or gentlemanly pursuits: walking deep in polite conversation, riding, collecting shells for nature study or pressing; or there were invalids gently inhaling ozone uncertain whether to take their complaints to Bath, as usual, or risk newfangled methods. The merits of brisk toning-up were obviously doubtful to him who described Teignmouth sands in about 1838 as: 'always firm and safe for riding and walking, with fine smooth sand when a southerly wind prevails — the only one during which an invalid has any business with the sea beach'.

73

Beach dignity: Brighton in 1846, before the introduction of deckchairs.

How similar lingering languishers shuddered behind their clean, harmless newspapers and novels, as more uninhibited seasiders passed, merry widows and hopeful swains among them, not only flaunting good health but disgusting disrespect for modesty, decency and the dear departed alike, as when Thomas Hood penned in about the year 1845:

> On Margate beach, where the rich one roams
> And the sentimental reads;
> Where the maiden flirts, and the widow comes —
> Like the ocean — to cast her weeds!

Blackpool, unawakened by the Wakes, was then more superior than Margate, presenting an archetypal example of sand life in a town untouched by trains yet already expanding, its wide beaches crowded with 'numerous groups and single individuals, scattered in all directions, some walking and others riding either on steeds or asses, dotting the extended strand which looks like the desert of Suez with the parted waters of the Red Sea murmuring at the distance'. Romanticised and fanciful? Some 250 miles south we can today see in effect what that Lancashire topographer saw. At Studland in Dorset is such a beach, fringed like the early Fylde coast by pale dunes and hummocks; photographs taken there in summer haze showing small ships entering Poole between spikes of grey reeds poking stiff as knitting needles from piled up sands, all rendered hotly pale by heat, do bear noticeable affinity with genuine Suez shots.

Blackpool or Studland, west or east; any coast was brush-fodder to the age when young ladies must be accomplished (another expression spoken as with capital letters); accomplished in dancing, music, singing, cookery, embroidery, pressing flowers and sketching. Carefully shaded by parasols and hats against the sun's threat of unladylike freckles, picturesque themselves in flowing white muslins and veiled white hats, they executed limp watercolours of uncontroversial subjects and still lifes of seaweed and shells. Not entirely to their taste was the earthy, masculine colour and movement of a certain gentleman seen working on canvas at Ramsgate, crowding his frame with massed figures and families; did not art masters preach that one soulful virgin holding a lily was Art but masses of everyday people doing everyday things vulgarity?

They dreamed not that, over a century after their proper, wishy-washy cameos were forgotten, his canvas would be recognised among the masterpieces of seaside painting, Frith's immortal *Ramsgate Sands*: nor could they imagine that the strange, introspective foreigner daubing loud colours two decades after at Ramsgate, between working as French teacher in a tiny local school and forays to London vainly trying to collect the boarders' fees, would join the immortals — the youthful Van Gogh.

Woman must paint like a woman, move like a woman, be fair of face, never freckled, and amuse herself femininely. That girls of the future would ride pillion on motorcycles, garbed in boots and crash helmets, was beyond reasonable ken, like imagining seaside donkeys flying. Riding horseback to hounds was admittedly permissible, side-saddle, but the notion of future women jockeys impossible; racing was a male sport for manly men, attended by ladies for social and fashionable reasons as onlookers.

Seaside racing was, for both riders and spectators, the sporting world's newest thrill as Scarborough changed over from spa to pleasure resort. In 1840 one writer enthusiastically described the beach, firm

Exquisite fashion seen at Littlehampton in about 1908.

Better-class children in sailor suits or muslins, allowed to mix with carriage goats if not with London charity children, at Littlehampton in about 1908.

enough for galloping hooves, as 'the course-ground and theatre of the equestrian as well as the pedestrian display of man's skill and animal agility', having joined an excited throng on the sensational new bridge for a dizzying view 'from a place suspended almost in the air'. Thus was racing enjoyed 'perhaps uniquely by the people of Scarborough, and the visitors, from the Cliff Bridge, which may indeed be said to be, on such an occasion, the grandest stand of any race ground in the world'. Equine speed on sand in 1840 was as thrilling as motor racing on Southport's specially firm beaches today.

Children, naturally, enjoyed the passing excitement of beach horse-racing, but otherwise their recipe for happiness was as it still is: buckets, spades, donkeys and time simply to sit, run and play. The chief difference between childhood on the strand in 1838, 1938 and 1978 was rather a matter of social contrasts. Now, most playing youngsters come of moderately-placed backgrounds, with poorer and richer fringe minorities according to resort. Then, the rich were ostentatiously rich as Solomon, too wealthy to enjoy themselves; the poor were truly poor but happy playing with sticks and catching crabs, enjoying one day at Brighton more than any pampered Honourable Priscilla her month at artificial Cannes; middle and upper-middle classes avoided both extremes of company, concerned chiefly that their offspring should not mix with East Enders' brats and 'catch something' which the school nurse might capture with her probing comb next term, inspiring rumours that the family was dirty. Spotty, tattered but possibly happiest in a miracle world of light, air and sand were parties of charity-children all alike in institutional frocks, smocks and white socks, sent thanks to wealthy philanthropists' donations or rescued by that bogey-man in reverse known to street parlance as 'the croolty-man' or child welfare inspector.

Undoubtedly all those classes enjoyed the beach more than poor little Priscilla, crimped, curled, dogged by nurses and governesses; even as the guns of another world war were being primed, enough Honourable Priscillas existed to justify continuance of such establishments as a Sussex Nursery Hotel, 'designed for Parents requiring a Home from Home for their Children, Governesses, and Nurses'.

Rich Priscilla sat on a hard church pew surrounded by grim, straight-backed aunts, twiddling her ringlets and wondering whether the sermonising clerical drone would ever reach Fifthly, Sixthly, Finally, Lastly, In Conclusion and Amen, whilst lucky Dora and Jane Smith escaped church or at least enjoyed the novelty of Sunday School outdoors on the sands that was destined to last beyond the doodle-bug

Sands across the sea, on a day trip to Ostend's beaches in 1898.

FRENCH AS SHE IS SPOKE.

"You like Ostende, Monsieur Simpkin?"

"Oh, yes, orfly! It's so 'richurch,' don'tcherknow. Just come up to the 'Curse Hall,' will you?"

age into the space-age itself; in the dark 1940s, the Salvation Army still kept its old wooden Sunday School forms permanently padlocked to Weston-super-Mare railings throughout summer, for holding of joyous clap-it-out chorus singing to uniformed bands under the Blood And Fire banner, for locals and evacuees forgetting by day Hitler's murder of Bristol by night; the same natural unforced religion that captured their grandparents by its cheerful assurance and sincerity. Similarly, at Worthing, at the time of writing, a Corporation notice on the beach still proclaims: 'Stand Appointed for the Delivery of Sermons, Lectures and Speeches' — another reminder that beaches for the past century have been combinations of chapel and Speakers' Corner in this blessed land of free speech.

Sunday School having dispersed, each child, whether in 1900 or 1940, or in the years between, returned to his family, singing *All Things Bright and Beautiful* slightly flat, to take up again his favourite pursuit, usually using something costing nothing but giving more pleasure than all the Honourable Priscilla's expensive dolls; objects such as broken sticks wherewith to inscribe 'John loves Mary — TRUE' or 'Nellie Jessop was here' in wet sand.

Adults were not above reverting to childhood in this respect, not least the Victorian writer Langhorne, meeting with the famous Somerset philanthropist and reformer, Hannah More, on Weston beach, where with his cane he cut the doggerel tribute:

> Upon this shore
> Walked Hannah More.
> Waves, let this record last!
> Sooner shall ye
> Proud earth and sea,
> Than what she writes, be past!

But of course the waves never let any record be, obliterating the celebrated lady's name with no more regret than Nellie's or John's when the tide rose.

High tide at Weston, Burnam, Grange-over-Sands, Southend or any place where waters retreated literally miles towards the horizon for hours, reducing the sea to a thin silver distant streak, was ever a thrill beyond the ken of Swanage or Worthing, where low water is never far out. Excitement lifted the spirits as distant mudbanks sank under ripples, and sea sounds crescendoed from a far murmur to a swish, a swoosh and finally a roar, as increasingly foamy waves approached, until paddling became possible. It was worth waiting four hours for the reality of Browning's 'warm, sea-scented beach'; less poetically, for smells of newly-deposited seaweed, designed by the wise Creator expressly for young feet to stamp upon and hear their large golden brown water-filled globules explode with audible pops. Mother, remembering her own infancy, took smaller seaweed festoons, dried and left by last tide, demonstrating how to pop their lumps and bumps by hand; done aright, this made satisfying noises and left ribbons of tiny deflated brown balloons, guaranteeing adults peace for ten whole minutes.

Seaweed, added father like a wise oracle, was tougher than it looked; strong enough for tug-of-war games if he deliberately disguised his strength against a small daughter's pulling hands. Daddies were also created to show where to find crabs, by upturning flat wet stones to watch the comic creatures scuttle sideways, but Mummies for drying tears when a young paddler flew howling from shallow waters at Southend, where myriads of tiny crabs, washed in by rising tides, floated and tickled around bare feet, not actually biting — but they might.

Why, when busy with Creation, did God stop to create such diverse objects as the braying, long-eared donkey, goats and seaside beaches? The answer in every child's mind, from the dawn of seaside holidays, was simple: sands were made for donkeys to give rides and goats to draw little carriages, loaded with laughing children.

Donkey rides, though not so ubiquitous as before 1939, are yet with us, but goat carriages are picturesque things of the past, met only in Victorian and Edwardian descriptive writing or fading but historically precious photo albums. It was said of Eld, Brighton's last dandified Master of Ceremonies before railway days: 'He approached the little goat carriages; he looked askance over the edge of his starched neckcloth, and blandly smiled encouragement.'

Present package tourists in Morocco and the Canary Islands find the sight of camels meekly kneeling to pick up passengers, rising to their knobbly but stately knees on command, sights to recount for months afterwards; but in England most children whose parents could afford seaside days were once familiar with the general principle, from watching the goat carts that are now history.

Fading sepia shows us a sailor-suited boy and his little sister in muslin hesitantly standing, dwarfed by the enormous upright horns of

Goat carts, popular transport at Bognor in 1926.

79

a harnessed pair of carriage goats, on the sands of Bognor (not yet Regis). Bigger, broader, taller and hornier than farmyard goats' horns, they dominate the picture, as the animals kneel together on the strand while children mount their light wooden cart. At neighbouring Little-hampton, always a juvenile paradise because sands are the heart and soul of childhood happiness, more ranks of goats stood patiently as the nineteenth century merged into the twentieth; some as large and deceptively ferocious as the beasts of Bognor, others smaller, darker-coated and, given tight reining and constant prodding, capable of a faster turn of speed.

A rowing boat that never went to sea at Bognor in 1926.

Ponies also did beach duty, trotting with less jerky muscular co-ordination, hauling novelty cartloads of young holidaymakers, often dressed up in storybook guise. At Bognor young Noël of the pathetic wartime postcards, grown now to sailor-suit age, bowled over smooth sands in a full-sized rowing boat that never went to sea, mounted on a low horse-drawn chassis. Weston-super-Mare, forced to emphasise beach attractions to compensate for its infuriating tide that retreated halfway to Wales all day and rose just as Mama decreed that it was time to go home, established several ranks of pony- and horse-drawn carriages with exciting themes that became its greatest source of beach fame and still exist in goodly numbers today: Cinderella's coach for little girls; Donald Duck, with seats in his back; dragons and battleships; aeroplanes and fire engines; comic paper characters and film ogres, according to period, mounted on the same rubber-tyred chassis but altered and repainted seasonally to follow current trends, right through to helicopters and Batman.

Donkey rides, however, showed little variation beyond the increasing liberation of the riders themselves from unchildlike confines of stays, laces, petticoats and bonnets towards light 1930s ginghams, via the inevitable sailor-suit period. Possibly the latter was photographically the most picturesque; Great-Grandpa's shaky hand on the shutter, or

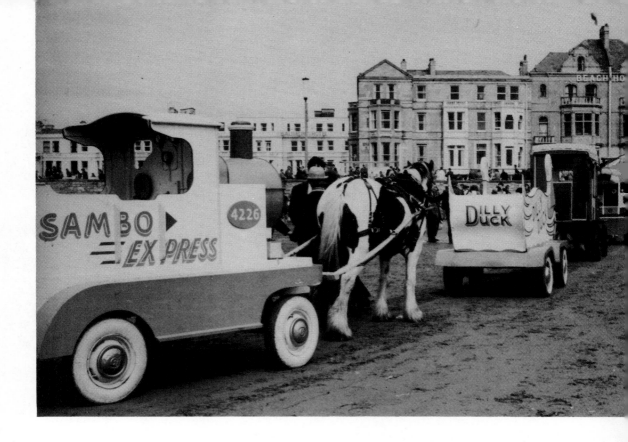

Twentieth-century fairy-tale coaches at Weston-super-Mare, descendants of generations of pony carts.

a schoolgirl with her cheap box camera, could not avoid producing pictures of exquisite retrospective charm, as Great-Grandmama posed in flowing filmy Edwardian white dress and hat, supporting her miniature boy sailor on his Littlehampton donkey.

Donkey-riding dates well before Great-Grandmama herself, to fine ladies religiously following George III's cult of ozone-breathing and less wealthy London maidens wafted to Margate by river, in whom local boatmen and donkeymen spotted potential trade, additional to fishing and illegal smuggling. As a scribe of 1820 commented of this increasingly profitable dual practice of both daylight labour and moonlighting, helped by faithful beasts impartially bearing two different burdens:

> ASSES HERE TO LET!
> For all purposes right!
> To bear Angels by day,
> And Spirits by night!

the spirits in question being brandy undeclared to prowling excise cutters.

Margate donkeys remained famous, long after smugglers found tourism more profitable, as did the asses of every resort blessed with sands instead of shingle. Burnham-on-Sea donkeys, more than anything else, filled slow steam trains on the single branch line from inland dairying Somerset, including regular Sunday School specials chartered entirely for village children from miles around, one village to each

81

IN DISTRESS.

"Mummy! Mummy! Come back! I'm frightened. Here's a horrid Dog *staring at me with his teeth!*"

carriage, pouring out in hundreds when the tiny tank engines gasped asthmatically to a halt only yards from the beach. Burnham Donkeys were Burnham, each with his name on a broad painted headband — Neddy, Big Ears Dolly, Smiley, Happy — moving off in droves of twenty or more together, carrying aunts unashamed to act briefly like children among them. To quote a typical postcard sent home to London 'Dear Daddy: can you see your little girl and her Auntie on the donkeys? . . . We have been here a week, and it hardly seems as long . . . . Renie said she wanted to go home today to see her Daddy [those were the days of husbands' boats, when fathers unentitled to paid holidays managed only to send their wives and children away, continuing breadwinning themselves] soon after this was taken, Auntie fell off.' Typical, also, is one revealing background detail of this beach-photographer's effort, rows of gapers and gawpers on the esplanade above, staring in fascination at the spectacle of filming outdoors without studio drapes and grimly-held exposures of seconds which seemed like face-aching hours.

Cashing in on beach leisure: a Clacton photographer of 1916 ensnares over forty watchers of his 'birdie' — and hopes to sell forty prints from just one negative.

Every child loved donkeys; very few meant cruelty when singing their favourite ditty about Long-Ears:

Hallelujah! Skin a donkey!
Cut 'is tail off!
Amen!

Not all appreciated how appropriate was an Amen to that otherwise undistinguished doggerel, unless Daddy or the donkeymen pointed out a curious natural fact about donkeys, by handing on a legend nearly two thousand years older than seaside holidays, as old as Biblical days. At mealtimes, when saddlery was removed while the animals tucked into fresh hay thrown into big wire baskets on the beach, the marks of legend were clearly revealed, particularly on light-coated asses; a long

Punch's view of the less placid aspects of beach life in 1898.

83

A DEGRADING THOUGHT.

Bertie. "WELL, SUSAN, IS THIS FAIR? WE WERE GOING TO PLAY AT LIONS AND SHEEP, AND THEY WANT *ME* TO BE A SHEEP AND *THEM* TO BE LIONS!"

unbroken ridge of darker coarse hair from neck to tail along the spine and a shorter band crossing it at the shoulder. No donkey, it would be told, was without that natural branding, dating from the earliest Palm Sunday when a humble ass carried its most distinguished passenger into Jerusalem, past cheering crowds waving palm fronds and throwing them under the donkey's clopping hooves, as he played a processional role usually reserved for dignified horses. When Jesus dismounted, there was the imprint of the Cross on his fur, foreshadowing events to come. Ever since, legend continues, all donkeys have been born with that furry sign. Kneeling beside a tiny foal, lying with its mother on Burnham beach, hearing this ancient story from a donkey man with a Zummerzet accent, a child would remember this until she herself had children.

Letting lunch go down: sunbathing in the 1930s wearing decent wintry hats.

Not for long does childhood keep quietly gentle. Whether in the days of velvet bonnets or faded gingham, beauty always changed to howling in the twinkling of a proverbial eye: 'Want to 'ave me pick-cher took!'; or 'Ma! I'm hungry!'; or a long unlovely 'Eeeeeoooaaahhh!', meaning cut feet on a stone or fragment of broken glass. Granny remedies soon settled the latter (Sanitary Rose Powder from a roomy black handbag, 'Invaluable to tourists and at the seaside etc., for Sunburn and Tender Feet'). With luck, request number one was cheaply completed by joining one of the massed groups shot by profiteers hopefully selling up to fifty copies of one print, prominently displayed and captioned IS *YOUR* CHILD HERE?

Picnicking and peace followed. Filling their faces was the surest way of keeping a boy quiet and his sister occupied.

'Children's Paradise' says the holiday advertisement; but even in paradise *Punch* finds it is infant nature to howl (1898).

Out came wicker hampers full of nourishing goodies. Even though Father's income was a miserly £3 a week and his brood numbered six, and though Mother as a result often made do with one apple for lunch

"HADN'T WE BETTER GO HOME, NURSE? I DON'T THINK THESE PIERROT SONGS ARE QUITE SUITABLE FOR BABY."

[The Bathing Season at Scarborough has commenced.]

TERRIBLE EXPERIENCE OF THE JENKINS FAMILY WHILST DRIVING ON THE SANDS. THE POSTILLION, WHO WAS, UNFORTUNATELY, SOMEWHAT DEAF AND ABSENT-MINDED, HAD, UNTIL QUITE RECENTLY, BEEN IN CHARGE OF A BATHING-MACHINE HORSE!

to save money, their offspring never went short. True, fresh ham was not on the menu but bread and cheese outdoors followed by dates, apples and lashings of Mother's 'piggy jam' (fig jam) tasted better to Will, Stan, Ray, Laura, Dolly and Nellie from an inland terraced street than all the meats and fruit consumed in gilded dining-rooms, supervised by starchy waiters and stiff governesses, by poor little rich Priscilla's kind. Bunfight was the proper word for a lively family repast, topped by ginger pop and lemonade.

So full were tummies invigorated by donkey rides and pure air that it needed not Mother's warning to 'let it go down' before safely bathing, to anchor her flock. They were all too ready simply to lie back, bury Auntie in sand up to her middle, or hear true stories about the very beach where they sat; of pirates, smugglers and local boys who went to sea and came back heroes; perhaps of how Captain Cook, intrepid penetrator into the uncharted Pacific and the Antarctic Circle, lived in a cottage facing the very harbour of Whitby where the family were resting; or how Redcar lifeboat, which they had seen only hours ago, descended directly from the oldest lifeboat in the whole world, the *Zetland*, saver of lives off Redcar from 1800.

After picnic time, crowds poured back from the hotels onto the beach, and the bedlam of minstrels and buskers, temporarily stilled while they ate, returned in fuller force than ever.

How insignificant by comparison are the worst uproars of modern seasides — transistor radios, youths with guitars, bingo-callers, cafe juke boxes and perhaps one band — against beach noises of yore. Numberless were the scrapers and blowers that Dickens of Broadstairs called 'most excruciating': German bands and Flemish troubadours; blaring trumpeters, and barrel organists; fiddlers alone or in groups, rarely in tune, scraping ancient instruments whose bows undoubtedly *were* strung with horsehair (with the neighing horse still attached) and whose strings demonstrated only too clearly why their material was named catgut; bell-ringers and shouting vendors; vagrants banging drums and singers who could not sing. Jane Carlyle, like Dickens, squirmed to their 'music' at the next resort along Kent's coastline, Ramsgate, when she wrote: 'A brass band plays all through our breakfasts, and repeats the performance often during the day, and is succeeded by a band of Ethiopians, and that again by a band of female fiddlers; and interspersed with these are individual barrel organs, Scotch bagpipes, and individual French horns.' Only the children thoroughly enjoyed this characteristic Victorian beach din, more so than ever when the Nigger Minstrel era dawned.

Their origin was American and their main ancestry the Virginian Minstrels whose style of programme became standardised everywhere; white singers and comedians, with exaggeratedly blacked faces and painted lips and eyes, in garish costume, plucking the banjo in imitation Negro songs and clicking primitive pairs of animal bones in

87

the fashion of castanets, from which developed the centrepiece act of Nigger minstrelsy, Mister Bones. Every English seaside had its minstrels, following suit, to which rapturous young audiences roared in response 'Mister BONES!', performing morning, afternoon and evening on the beach. Frith's *Ramsgate Sands* clearly shows them in action.

Later came the age of concert parties, more mixed entertainment akin to the Halls, with singers, dancers and clownlike frilled pierrots, performing outdoors by day and in pier pavilions by night; many were composed entirely of one versatile family, ranging from a properly-trained young dancer performing Pavlova's latest solo in satin pointe-shoes, tutu and curls to female trumpeters and jugglers. Perhaps most famous of all beach entertainers was Uncle Mack of Broadstairs; right up to 1937, long after Dickens' hated tumult and trumpeting had died, he was delighting grandchildren of his first audiences, after fifty years.

Not only did theatre, Music Hall and concert parties come onto the beach. The beach, as if returning the compliment, went into the theatre. Who did not know that once popular ditty of a garishly dressed, bookie-type London tradesman?

> The weather was hot and trade was slow,
> So to Margate I resolved to go,
> On the sands, on the sands, on the sands.

> In a light tweed suit that fitted me well,
> I went down for a week, a first class swell,
> On the sands, on the sands, on the sands.

At the seaside, theatre for everyone between two and the teens has always meant a miniature stage and proscenium with puppet actors, squeaky or growling comic voices and a gruesome ending, played from an upright booth, round which the audience sat on benches or plain sand, with open mouths and bated breath, no matter how many times they had seen the same short drama acted out before: Punch and Judy.

No sooner did society adopt the bathing ritual, before transport even took to steam, than some of London's many Italian Punch and Judy men took the same road, sensing better profits in sons and daughters of rich men than in poor city street urchins. 'Watering places is werry good in July and August' responded a team interviewed by a leading social researcher of the early 1850s; 'Punch mostly goes down to the seaside, with the quality; Brighton, though, ain't of no account; the Pavilion's done up with, and therefore Punch has discontinued his visits'; instead Punch sought fresh beaches at Merry Margate or Little-hampton, the children's Paradises. The quality, in any case, had proved less profitable than expected, thanks to the craftiness of nursemaids lining their own pockets: 'Nusses ain't no good; even if the mothers of the dear children has given 'em a penny to spend, why the nusses takes it from 'em, and keeps it for ribbins.' Poor kids' pennies, pressed directly into the

Beach donkey: legends of a donkey and Palm Sunday were always favourites among stories told on seaside beaches.

'I spy with my little eye . . .' bare feet and quite four inches of bare ankle were permissible by about 1908 — so long as a lady wore heavy suiting and a close hat in midsummer.

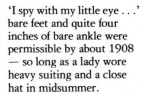

operator's hand, found their rightful destination, because personally paying Punch was half a boy's fun. The other half, of course, was bawling at Punch, his wife, the policeman or Toby, pantomime fashion, through to the 'Second H'act' climax of 'Dead! Dead! Dead!' and the horrible triple sentence 'for killing your wife, throwing your dear little innocent baby out of the window, and striking the Beadle unmercifully over the head with a mop-stick'. The gallows was the supreme ecstasy of Punch and always would be.

Once Punch was over, young feet became as active as ever, rushing in and out of sparkling waves, fetching buckets of water for filling the moats of sand castles, from the crumbling keeps of which big brothers taunted:

> I'm the king of the castle,
> Get down, your dirty rascal!

Sandcastle competitions were major features of inter-war beach life officially organised in such large resorts as Llandudno with worthwhile prizes. Men, always small boys inside their city pin-stripes, could cast off pretence and *be* small boys; boys with experience, engineering skill and building knowledge capable of executing remarkable masterpieces in wet sand, from Windsor Castle with all its battlements and chapels, to engines and trains, paddle-steamers big enough to sit inside and fantastic dragons more than worthy of their awards. Only a few precision sandcastle makers continue today, notably a gentleman of Weymouth, whose creations occasionally catch the eye of the press.

Child or man, beginner or expert, a sandcastle-builder's handiwork was doomed within hours. Tides, like time, waited for neither. Down crumbled those elaborate battlements and turrets, and the moat filled with unwanted floodwater. Daddy's hour of childhood was over, leaving him to meditate again in his deckchair, hastily dragged higher up the beach against advancing waves, upon the subject of Saturday; Saturday which seemed to be rushing towards him faster than the waves upon the disappearing sandcastle, posing Lamb's old unanswerable question:

> Who first invented Work? And tied the free
> And holiday rejoicing spirit down
> To the everlasting importunity
> Of business? . . .

Johnny and Jane as yet cared nothing. Saturday was two days away, a long time in a ten-year-old's reckoning. Boats, formerly stranded on wet mud, were jerking upright on deepening seas, masts bobbing on gentle wavelets; sunshine dazzled on enlarging breakers; seaweed straggled and floated around paddling feet, tickling deliciously. Had they known, or cared, who Dickens was, they surely would have preferred his conception to Lamb's harsh words of reality: 'Confused timber defences against the waves lie strewn about in a brown litter of seaweed and fallen cliff . . . . The tide has risen; the boats are dancing on bubbling water; the colliers are afloat again; the white-bordered waves rush in.'

'With one consent to rush into the sea': a card sent from Blackpool in George V's reign.

7. Bathing-Machines and Bloomers

Two inventions — one inanimately wooden, one made animate by action of human limbs inside — will ever be synonymous with seaside life between the Third and Fifth Georges: the bathing-machine, within which modesty dictated a lady must change from walking to watering dress; and the bloomers which, in one outrageous stroke of fashion, blew conceptions of modesty apart, letting in successive eras of exposed ankles, then knees and one-piece bathing-suits actually designed for bathing.

> All, impatient of dry land, agree
> With one consent to rush into the sea.

Cowper's couplet aptly portrays that period when Society, drifting from inland spas, first trundled itself within horse-drawn Noah's arks into shivery waves, following George III's example which made Weymouth 'the first seaside resort where ladies and gentlemen of fashion could in propriety indulge in the newly recommended practice of seabathing'. Bathing-machines were propriety's very basis, enabling well-bred women swathed in layers of fashionable dry clothing complete with corsetry to be drawn into shallow water and descend on the seaward side protected by the machine itself, plus attendant women, from prying eyes. Weymouth prided itself on some of the earliest machines in England, even before any royal toe was dipped into its waters, thanks to 'the public spirited action of several residents including Ralph Allen, formerly of Bath, the original of Fielding's Squire Allworthy', for whom one was built in 1763; a wheeled shed so heavy that carthorses could scarcely drag it across Weymouth sands. More appeared, enabling Allen's expensive gouty Bath friends, brought by resplendent carriages, to immerse themselves in the briney currently said to be as beneficial as Bath waters themselves. Fashion, characteristically, followed fashion like the creatures behind Noah: husbands and wives, dukes and duchesses, earls and countesses, squires and matrons, two by two, not to escape Noah's original flood but to revel in flooding tides. Given a benediction by the Duke of Gloucester and finally by George III in 1789, bathing was established in perpetuity.

Weymouth became Bath-on-Sea, its 'vast concourse of polite company' being but Beau Nash's 'Polite Company' of Bath migrated from pump-room to bathing-machine. Everybody of standing thenceforth bathed; even Doctor Johnson, no Adonis undressed and minus velvet clubland garb, hence his pleasure in a Brighton bathing

TIDE COMING IN FAST. AND A JIBBING HORSE!

A perennial problem of the bathing-machine era — tide coming in fast, and a jibbing horse!

attendant's peculiarly backhanded compliment: 'Why, sir, you must have been a stout-hearted gentleman forty years ago!'

Characters with a capital C were eighteenth- and nineteenth-century bathing attendants. Two at least gained modest immortality through recorded exchanges between themselves and their distinguished charges, with whom no other working-class persons could expect to become so intimately involved. Martha Gunn, head bathing-woman of Brighton into extreme old age, headed the list, born of tough fishwife stock continuing in several generations of descendants after she dipped her last fine lady. 'Well and hearty, thank God, sir, but rather hobbling; I don't bathe now because I ain't so strong as I used t'be; so I superintend on the beach, for I'm up afore any of 'em; you may always find me and my pitcher at one exact spot, every morning by six o'clock,' was game old Martha's reply to one aristocratic enquirer. Nor was she coy when further questioned on her age: 'Only eighty-eight sir; in fact, eighty-nine come next Christmas pudding; and though I've lost me teeth, I can mumble it with as good relish and hearty

92

appetite as anybody.' Hard work and sheer pride in being personally greeted by almost everyone from princesses downwards kept Martha going: 'While I've life and health, I must be bustling among my old friends and benefactors; I think I ought to be proud, for I've had as many bows from man, woman and child as the Prince hisself; aye, and I do believe the very dogs in the town know me.' Without question they did.

Martha's male counterpart was John Miles, known to all as Smoaker, swimming instructor to the young Prince of Wales. Conscious of total responsibility for an Heir to the Throne, Smoaker was reputedly not above dragging the Prince back by his ear for swimming too far out. Nor did he feel compelled to address him unduly softly: 'What do you think your father would say to me if you were drowned?' roared enraged Smoaker, threatening the royal youth with clenched fists; 'He would say, "This is all owing to you, Smoaker; if you'd taken proper care of him, Smoaker, poor George would still be alive".' Smoaker's vigilance ensured that George lived to ascend many more times the contraption thus described in a Brighton handbook of 1794. 'By means of a hook-ladder, the bather ascends the machine, which is formed of wood and raised on high wheels; he is drawn to a proper distance from the shore, and then plunges into the sea, the guides attending on each side to assist him in recovering the machine which being accomplished, he is drawn back to the shore.' Theoretically, he should have felt better for his plunge, particularly if he heeded the advice of Doctor Russell, father of Brighton bathing cures, to 'drink half a pint of seawater at five o'clock each morning, and then plunge his body beneath the waves'.

Was mortifying the flesh at such hours the ungodliest pursuit ever practised on Britain's beaches? Tight-lipped spinsters with sharp, half-outraged, half-fascinated eyes for goings-on disagreed; the ultimate in ungodly pursuits was not the hour at which man rose to swim, but the condition in which he did so — nude as a huge baby, in startling contrast to womankind, dragged dangerously down by folds of concealing fabrics over tight corsets.

Had she appreciated the underlying embarrassment of the men, whom custom dictated should swim nude, Miss Prim might have felt sympathy instead. Pleasure was considerably reduced by initially venturing out onto a bathing-machine's steps trussed up like a contortionist to preserve decency. Benjamin Beale of Margate, a Quaker in tune with Miss Prim, but also with shivering Mr Nude Bather, supplied the answer in about 1790: the famous modesty-hood.

Beale, sometimes erroneously credited with the invention of bathing-machines themselves instead of only this clumsy addition, reputedly ruined himself financially, fighting for recognition of his invention, but opened fortune's gateway to others who adopted and improved upon it. He also ruined Miss Prim's self-imposed righteous watchdog duty of

AN AQUATIC TEA-

stationing herself strategically on the beach (Bible in hand on Sundays) to destroy masculine swimmers' relaxation, sitting ramrod-backed on her stool so near their machines that it required considerable nerve for any man, marooned nude in the waves, to regain the ladder. Rumour spoke of a close relation, Miss Prude, beneath whose outward prudery ran psychological contradictions repressed tighter than her own lips, not above observing and reporting cases of indecency spied from clifftops through a telescope. She need not have caused herself such distress; but in Right's cause, she endured.

Modesty-hoods effectively blindfolded Miss Prim and Miss Prude; outsized billowing striped umbrellas, or canvas affairs in hinged sections, like gigantic babies' pram hoods, extended over a bathing-machine's ladder to sand level, entirely concealing descending men. Beale's successors, if not Beale himself, did excellent business with machines trailing ever larger modesty-shields, demanding not only fees but tips in their advertising: 'For Bathing in the Sea at Margate, John and Mercy Sayer, late partners with Mr Beale, have good accommodations for Bathing; Favours confer'd upon them will be Gratefully Acknowledg'd. Mr Sayer will attend ye Gentlemen, and Mrs Sayer ye Ladies' ran exhortations to use 'Sayers' Machine', portrayed with clumsy hinged hood being hauled to shore by one overburdened pony.

Emerging resorts everywhere considered their status in terms of bathing-machines rather than other amenities as the nineteenth century dawned, as a typical exhaustive survey of 1813 reveals. Little is said of Southwold, among many pages of history, beyond that 'it has of late years derived some benefit from the strangers who resort thither during the summer season . . . and for whose accommodation two convenient machines are kept in the town.' Bognor was 'a place which owes its existence to the prevailing rage for seabathing; so lately as 1784 it was known only as a resort for smugglers, and consisted merely of a few fishermens' huts', though nearby Worthing, surprisingly, boasted sixty bathing-machines. Almost all that could be said of Lowestoft, among twenty-two pages of kipper-curing and church history, was that 'four bathing machines are kept for the use of The Company, by whom this place has of late years been much frequented during the Season.'

Little more could be said of Hastings and Eastbourne, but royal Brighton was a different story, 'possessing every possible convenience for seabathing', plus cliff walks, promenades and donkeys (the ponies of Biblical lands) for rich girls to ride whilst Father laboured on in his City bank:

> Phoebus the tanner plies his fiery trade,
> The graceful nymphs ascend Judea's ponies;
> Scale the West Cliff, or visit the Parade,
> While poor Papa in Town a patient drone is.

Previous pages: Brighton continues the bathing that made it famous from Prinny's day; a cartoon from 1881.

Beale's bathing-machine at Margate advertised in 1791.

Serious bathing, for health instead of sport, required early rising, inner and outer cleanliness by courtesy of Mother Ocean, and the mentality of a spa patron, according to such preachers as the 'celebrated Doctor Crane' of Weymouth.

The most proper time for bathing is early in the morning, fasting, before which no exercise should be taken, more especially in hot weather, which will cause great depression of spirits. Perfect repose of body and serenity of mind are absolutely necessary to promote the purposes of this great remedy.

Bathing among companies as genteel as at many spas required increasingly strict regulations, additional to modesty-hoods, such as a statutory three or four minutes' walking space between groups of ladies' and gentlemen's bathing-machines and careful control of prospective Peeping Toms; five shillings fine, a large sum then, was Southport's price for boats straying within spying distance of ladies, which wealthy daredevils allegedly occasionally paid willingly for the sport of zooming into forbidden waters; considering that only floating shapeless masses of heavy black or blue flannel were visible, except from chin level upwards, their money bought precious little excitement.

Excitement ran far higher for the girls themselves in certain resorts where stony, shifting beaches, hard on feet in dainty slippers, replaced sands, notably at Brighton. Being carried by a handsome hunk of bathing-attendant across rough shingle, squealing naughtily if his clasp became closer than safety demanded, was Brighton's delight and scandal, according to whether one were young and irresponsible or elderly and sour. As was observed in about 1839:

97

Bathing-machines in regiments at Westcliff, near Southend-on-Sea, in about 1916.

The ladies who used the machines on the beach at Kemptown, seemed to prefer being carried to their distant, and almost floating, *cabinets-des-bains*, in the brawny arms of stout, broad shouldered fellows engaged for that purpose. It would be ludicrous, if it were not somewhat indecent, to behold how fast these modern Naiads cling to their lusty Neptunes while the latter hurry through the waves with their fair cargoes, until they deposit them in the floating bathroom, where a female attendant is at hand to help and guide them in and out of the water; such a practice, however (much as it may be deemed objectionable), the dangerous appearance of the shore in this place would almost seem to sanction.

'Well dressed is suitably dressed, dear' was the middle- to upper-class Grandmama's favourite maxim, drummed into frivolous passing generations as fashion moved towards the horrors of dresses without hoops, looser stays, bloomers, divided skirts and, in the futuristic 1920s, one-piece bathing suits exposing whole legs plus parts of backs.

Being well dressed when Brighton belles were carried seawards by Brighton beaux meant enveloping oneself in flannel which, instead of clinging provocatively to lovely forms like the shifts worn in spas' ripple-less waters, ballooned unbecomingly as bathers, lowered by the attendants or dippers, encountered eddying currents. Nor were clothes for beach lounging more comfortable; stiff, non-draping woollen folkweaves, made on handlooms at home by 'kept' daughters between sewing Papa's intricately tucked shirts.

Bathing in Victoria's early years was duty rather than pleasure, 'a luxury to the healthful, but a restorative to the sick'. Seawater continued to be regarded as a medicine, 'mixed with port wine, milk or beef-tea to make it more palatable' for victims of anything from measles to St Vitus' dance. Kill or cure? That question readily comes to minds regarding such tantalisingly incomplete resort epitaphs as

'Thomas Wood, Formerly a Bather at this Place' (Margate); or, to one who probably over-zealously followed bathing with the recommended brisk walk and cliff climb, again in Thanet:

> Against his will, here lies George Hill,
> Who from a cliff fell down quite stiff;
> When it happen'd 'tis not known,
> Therefore not mention'd on this stone.

Changing opinion as Victoria matured implanted seeds destined to germinate into present ideas of bathing purely for enjoyment instead of duty, speaking against older principles of 'forcing people in for their health . . . because they think it a duty if they go to the seaside'; but being Suitably Dressed continued to imply becoming almost dangerously waterlogged rather than reveal one naked ankle, if feminine, whatever might be permissible in rough, uncouth man. Suitable Dress was thick pantaloons, encumbrances of tight winter-weight dresses trimmed military style with braid, and strangulating underpinnings of bone and leather, until in about 1849 a daring costume became acceptable, laced as usual to the chin and corseted beneath, but stopping disgracefully short of the knees.

Knees! Calves! Ankles! Miss Prim's and Miss Prude's successors pursed scandalised lips as younger ladies frolicked in seawater, heralding new eras of freedom for limbs, bodies and minds. Had they known of the next fashion foible in advance, their lips must have become thinner in line than a strand of cotton.

Gazing horizonwards from Cornish beaches as the 1848 season progressed, pondering that nothing lay between himself and America, none but a prophet could have forecast what fashions lay beyond that horizon, born of early feminist stirrings, the Womens' Rights Movement, whose outward symbol of sexual equality was a mannish costume. Amelia Bloomer improved upon it almost immediately with the unisex outfit — male from the waist down, female from waist to neck — eternally to bear her name; the Bloomer suit of tailored but attractive jacket, knee-length skirt and comfortable, full, billowing trousers in Turkish style allowing a completely new range of feminine leg movements in recreation, the famous Bloomers.

Wearing Bloomers required too much courage to become universal, yet they made sufficient impact to alter for good existing conceptions of suitability in dress for increasingly sporty womankind, paving the way towards the Naughty Nineties and worse. Bloomers even invaded the ultra-masculine domain of trains by the 1880s, through a variety of locomotive which had exposed instead of ironclad 'legs', or driving wheels, known for that reason as Bloomer Class. Sister engines of slightly smaller wheel diameter predictably became Small Bloomers, differentiated from a handful of models sporting huge driving wheels taller than the tallest man, railway history's delightfully nicknamed Extra Large Bloomers. Have such a feminine creature as a Society

Suitably dressed and suitably hatted, for it is still 1920 — but the lady dares to show one ankle, albeit coyly.

99

THE BATHING QUESTION.

MASTER TOMMY IS EMPHATICALLY OF THE OPINION THAT THE SEXES OUGHT *NOT* TO BATHE TOGETHER.

100

Everybody bathed, even baby, here pictured in the shadow of a bathing-machine's wheels in about 1899.

bather and so masculine a monster as an early steam engine been linked before or since by the common factor of an item of semi-underwear?

Returning to an ever repeated theme, that there is nothing new under the sun, we find the Naughty Nineties continuing what today calls unisex fashion, not only through bloomers and divided skirts but at the opposite anatomical extreme, in headgear. Rare old negatives leave one in almost as much doubt as today in deciding which are girls and which boys, when both sport quasi-military caps and pillboxes or the ubiquitous sailor hat.

Everybody bathed, and every place with a modicum of tidal water called itself a resort, including ambitious All Hallows on Kent's estuary marshes, never truly to develop until the caravanning 1960s, and Gravesend, cowering shamefacedly a few more miles up Thames, no seaside at all geographically yet gamely keeping up with the Margate and Southend Joneses: 'There is a varied and interesting (though not very clean or fragrant) walk by the shore to Rosherville . . . . Eastwards are bathing machines and bathing establishments', wallowing in the muddy wakes of passing shipping. Everybody bathed, because everybody swore bathing was 'good for yer'; to quote Nineties' music hall patter: 'Bathing strengthens the h'interlect, braces the body, clears the system, puts new life in the blood . . . cures corns, warts, bunions, Pilgrims Progress, water on the brain, NEWralgia, OLDralgia, velocipedes, bicycles, tellerphones, tellergrams, and all the Primrose ''Ills wot the flesh is heir to''.'

A new monarch on the throne, Edward the uninhibited Seventh, heralded the twentieth century and greater tolerance of once taboo practices. Bathing-machines galore characterised every resort ('A glance at the beach at the height of the season would certainly give the impression that bathing was the one occupation of a holiday at Weymouth,' rhapsodised a 1907 guidebook), but machines now had less decent rivals, notably hired or bought tents, from which bathers boldly trod across sands instead of being hauled by horses into all-covering waters. 'The bathing is excellent,' it was said of Lyme Regis, 'though the machines are not of modern design. If one does not care for the striped, parti-coloured boxes, one can take a tent on wheels for the matutinal dip.' Similarly at Weymouth, 'visitors may, on payment to the Corporation of a nominal sum, erect their own tents on the sands' or one of those 'hired cheaply on the beach or in the town'. Buying one's own tent was a pricey business; a miniature circus big-top 'providing comfort and convenience for seaside pleasures' was advertised at 66/6 (£3.32½p decimalised), the average Papa's weekly pay.

Bathing-costumes and towels, too, were customarily hired out, up to the eve of the Second World War, usually black, baggy and shapeless, coming in only three sizes, Small, Medium and Large, and

The latest daring fashion on a typical *Punch* battleaxe of 1898.

101

High jinks and daringly low necklines in the fashionably emancipated naughty period.

inscribed in white to prevent pilferage '. . . Corporation'. Conceptions of decency changed rapidly, allowing ladies to show entire ankles whilst paddling, so long as a coy, half-brave and half-embarrassed smile was also worn, and children to display calves and knees, so long as heads were covered, in the cruellest heatwave, by sailor hats.

A lady — any female between nineteen and ninety — was as yet no lady if she returned from Southport or Morecambe to Manchester's suburbs flaunting a suntan, after carelessly throwing off her hat or parasol, or forgetting to use Kalydor For The Skin ('Cooling, Refreshing, Soothing to the Face and arms in Hot Weather; prevents Freckles, Tan, Sunburn, Redness, Roughness . . . makes the skin beautifully soft and white and imparts a Marvellous Beauty to the complexion unobtainable by any other means'). Neither was a lady a lady if she abandoned stays on holiday, even for bathing; hence the enthusiasm of this Welsh fashion copy-writer offering corsets boned to resist rusting by seawater at Rhyl or Colwyn Bay.

When you are on a Holiday you naturally desire freedom from all Dress Worries . . . facility of movement and thorough Ease. Nothing annoys a Woman so much as the snapping of a Corset steel as the result of a little extra Exertion. The 'Oktis' prevents all this and DOUBLES THE LIFE OF YOUR CORSET, and it CANNOT POSSIBLY RUST your Underclothing as it contains Rustless . . . stiffeners.

And a lady in loud bright barmaid colours was similarly no lady. Good breeding, whether genuine or assumed annually before one's hotel companions, decreed cream or white for strolling or demure pale blues and greens and the delicate frilled and flounced shades of pink that inspired lower-bred urchins to chant:

> Nasty Pink
> It makes you stink,
> And spoils the look of you!

Fabric now had to be thin and floating, far removed from Great-Great-Grandmama's home-woven stiff skirts, so fragile that young Johnny Bloggs' instinctive reaction was, 'Cor! You could shoot peas through *that*!' proving or disproving the point with his peashooter, or nearly giving the lady heart failure with a clever cheap toy emitting a sound exactly like expensive muslin being torn, let off behind her stately back.

World war in all its horror was well behind those who came, saw and bathed in the 1920s briney, and emancipation of women, far beyond Great-Great-Grandmama's imagining, was well under way; yet old-fashioned orders clung to the English seaside, including bathing-machines and tents. 'The bathing-machines are well appointed; mixed bathing is very popular . . . permission to erect private tents may be obtained from the Town Clerk,' announced Eastbourne. Seaford inclined towards the type of bathing-tent still available today. 'Instead of the common "Noah's Ark" machines, there are light tents with a grated floor, and by payment of a nominal sum the right to erect a private tent can be acquired.' The mid-1920s additionally offered a cross between the two, wooden huts like bathing-machines, entered by steep steps, but anchored firmly ashore at the back of the beach; in appearance, real-life versions of Gilbert's classic:

> Something between a large bathing machine,
> And a very small second-class carriage.

Dress became positively daring, though grandmas often clung rigidly to old-fashioned parasols and wore tall stovepipe hats with fur-collared coats against the tiniest puff of wind on summery days. Younger life coined Sporty Old Chap fashions — striped blazers, flannels and perky hats. Black one-piece bathing suits, edged with white, with plunging necklines, appeared on Corporation hire, as well as privately-owned versions, encouraging young Bloggs to comment of Grandpa's chest, exposed by a bathing-suit one size too big, blazoned in white 'Herne Bay Corporation': 'Cor! I've seen better hairs on bacon!'

Ladylike yet revealing: a bathing costume of the 1920s.

103

Over-sized hired suit.

The 1930s brought ginghams and hatless heads to English beaches, and skirts touched knees for younger women, though Auntie stuck to calf length and Granny to just above her ankles. Men's hired bathing costumes continued to be black but were sometimes daringly worn off one shoulder, having only one single strap, quite as disgraceful in stick-in-the-mud eyes as a younger cousin's cleavage.

Margate opened its fine new Bathing Pavilion, replacing bathing-machines to which, being well off-shore, patrons were formerly conveyed by horse and cart to shouts of 'Any more for the shore, please? And don't forget the driver.' Clacton went one better with a £60,000 pool with a novel system of lighting the water from below the surface for bathing at night; whilst in Devon, Paignton lured visitors with a precursor of water-skiing: 'Water polo is played, and bathers in search of novel pastimes can indulge in Paignton's speciality, plank-riding . . . . The planks on which the bather balances himself by means of a guiding rope, are drawn rapidly along the sea by motor boats.'

Bathing-machines were dead or dying, and modern amusements being born, as the Second World War loomed, as yet no larger than the Biblical cloud the size of a man's hand, on our seaboard horizons.

Three faces of 1920s fashion: long, calf length, young and brazen.

8. *Feeding Their Faces*

Certain foods and drinks, never seen on Mansion House or Grand Hotel menus, have been for some 150 years what popular speech terms seasidey: cockles, whelks and mussels; shrimps and lobster; ginger beer or pop and lemonade; ale and beer; home-boiled sweets; pie and chips; tripe and onions; candy floss and rock. Above all, seaside rock.

Hearty appetites ('apple-tights' in Victorianese) characterised British seasiders long before holidays in our modern sense arose, particularly down-Thames at Margate, Batholomew Fair by the Seaside, a favourite Londoners' resort despite a twelve-hour passage under sail if they were lucky, twice as long if they were not. Thus wrote Evelyn in 1672: '19th: Went to Margate . . .this Towne much consists of Brewers of a certaine Heady Ale, and they deale much in Malte'.

Prinny's Brighton was one round of sumptuous repasts, based on appetites made keener through sport and sea air. Dish followed dish, drink followed drink, from the cavernous kitchens whose very size gives present tourists some idea of the Pavilion's scale of catering; fish and Southdown lamb; poultry and venison from Windsor; lashings of cream, chocolate and exotic fruits, all washed down with wine and song. The MP who confessed such excesses of richness a bore was in a minority of one, but even he could not deny how merry good food made the company and the Prince, who 'behaved with the greatest good humour . . . anyone would have said that he was really a happy man'.

Happy, too, were rich dandies and richer City bankers, trailing strings of mistresses or daughters in their wakes accordingly, men and women fond of the table and willing to endure ever more rigorous corseting rather than diet, of whom some wag wrote in about 1813:

> Here with choice food Earth smiles, and Ocean yawns,
> Intent alike to please the London glutton;
> *This*, for our breakfast, proffers shrimps and prawns,
> *That*, for our dinner, South Down lamb and mutton.

Even religion and food were intertwined in Sussex, where on Whit Sunday pious countryfolk traditionally fed on veal and gooseberry pudding and a child born on a Sunday was said never to hang or drown.

Fish was a mainstay of both diet and trade at this period along the east coast, rather than the only half-awakened bathing trade, as at Aldborough (Aldeburgh), 'long famous . . . and abundantly supplied with every necessity and most of the luxuries of the table . . . herrings

Brighton Royal Pavilion as 'Prinny' knew it, scene of lavish banquets and suppers.

and sprats in large quantities . . .'; or at Lowestoft, dedicated to curing herrings rather than consumptive society beauties.

The principal part of the commerce of Lowestoft is derived from the herring fishery . . . . As soon as the herrings are brought on shore they are carried to the fish houses, and laid on the floors in heaps about two feet deep. After they have remained in this state about fifty hours, they are put into baskets and plunged into water to wash the salt from them. Wooden spits about four feet long are then run through the gills of as many of the fish as they will hold, and fixed at proper distances in the upper part of the house, as high as the top of the roof. A number of small wood fires, according to the size of the place, are kindled upon the floor, and by the smoke ascending from them the herrings are cured. After the fish have hung in this manner about seven days, the fires are extinguished for two days, that the oil and fat may drip from them. The fires are then rekindled and, after two more such drippings, they are kept continually burning until the fish are completely cured.

To this day, kippered herrings remain a favourite holiday breakfast food, notably near Blackpool and Fleetwood and on the Isle of Man.

Railway days brought huge increases in numbers patronising seaside resorts and a corresponding number of cashers-in to places either awakened or about to awake to tripper crowds. 'The cost of living, in every article, is about 33 per cent more than in London,' a Brighton sojourner wrote in 1839; 'Meat and fish are never sold during the Season at less than a penny or three halfpence a pound above London price; the tea and wine were represented to me as being of a very inferior quality, and yet sold at high prices . . . . Now this state of things cannot long endure after the railroad shall have come into operation.' In practice, of course, extortionists remained on the scene, joined by their cousins the landladies, who thought nothing of cramming six impecunious Londoners into one bedstead; 'little comfort, and poor food' were the cost of a breath of genuine ozone. Nathaniel Hawthorne, the novelist, summed up a sneaking suspicion on cottage pie that persists even into our modern day, 'the idea that you have eaten the scraps of other peoples' dinners'. Some mothers and grannies never lost their cottage pie complexes, instilling into new generations the reflex action of looking for bacon rind and beef gristle at the table. For them the ideal answer proved to be 'rooms' with catering.

She. "WHAT A MAGNIFICENT SUNSET! HOW IT LIFTS ONE'S THOUGHTS ABOVE THE EARTH!"

He. "AH, THAT REMINDS ME. YOU MIGHT SPEAK TO THE LANDLADY ABOUT OUR BACON IN THE MORNING. TELL HER I LIKE IT STREAKY."

Tongue in cheek: *Punch* catches romantic wife and mundane husband at the seaside.

At leisure on the beach in 1890.

Regional dishes were, on the contrary, much relished and taken into home cooks' repertoires on returning: Lancashire hotpot, a mainstay of Victorian kitchen economy; Cornish pasties; Devonshire dumplings; Cornish figgy squabs; Northumberland tanzy pudding or pan haggerty; Lancashire parkin; and dishes based on Zummerzet zoider.

Every region had such dishes, often known widely beyond its boundaries; Lancashire hotpot was as popular with London mothers on shoestring budgets as Leigh-on-Sea cockles with families 'feeding their faces' on promenades miles away. Some 80 per cent of all cockles eaten came, and still come, from Leigh near Southend, brought ashore from picturesque smacks crewed by grandsons and great-grandsons of Leigh cocklers, hauled ashore in a manner as old as nursery rhymedom itself, in heavy dripping baskets slung from the shoulders on milkmaids' wooden yokes. In timber sheds foggy with steam cockles were boiled, for sale outside picturesque pubs to Cockneys come down to do *Knees Up* on the quays and forget for one day their crowded tenements and claustrophobic factories. The beach itself was made of cockle shells, as it is today, a fine creamy white powder appearing at first sight to be sand, the top strata of generations of ground-up shells. Visitors' songs plugged the food aspect of happy days out, not only the traditional *Cockles and Mussels* but such handed-down doggerel as:

> Look at our Nellie
> Full up with jelly

108

to a popular operatic air and its tailpiece:

> Full up with ginger beer
> And monkey nuts.

Grandpas gathered wherever fish stalls abounded to invest in a dish utterly fascinating to their grandchildren; winkles, bought by the enamel mugful and individually picked from their shells with small sharp pins. Whelks closely vied with winkles in popularity, notably opposite Leigh on the Kentish shores; Herne Bay beach, it seemed to a child, was constructed half of pebbles and half of winkle shells swept in on the tide.

Shrimps, likewise bought by the pint or beaker, have always been a universal seaside favourite, though the chief source of their supply a century ago was not a seaport but our old friend the resort that was not really a resort, Gravesend, explaining why over a million visitors landed there in one season during the 1850s 'Shrimps are taken in prodigious quantities by the Gravesend fishermen,' it was recorded in 1875; 'They are very largely consumed at Gravesend by the summer visitors — there are whole streets of tea and shrimp houses — but the main dependence of the fishermen is on the London market.' Today the shrimps and bathing-machines have gone, but Gravesend preserves

Elegance at rest: the bikini age seems a million years away from 1872.

109

'Feed them up!' War wounded get preferential treatment, a Great War cartoon with a deeper meaning.

the best riverside gardens and promenades on the lower Thames, in memory of its great tripper days.

Eel pies and jellied eels were another universal platter, well patronised at the Thames 'seasides', notably Greenhithe yet further upstream, whose Victorian streets were lines with stalls dispensing 'Hot Eels and Pea Soup' while, in the same town, Mr Tiffin and his son plied their useful trade for the non-deodorised but heavily dressed ladies of Town, as 'Bug Destroyers to Her Majesty and the Royal Family'.

Certain eating places, like eatables themselves, belong to seaside days and ways: wooden kiosks, cliff teahuts, tea gardens, pier toffee, apple stalls and picnics on the sands or among spiney reeds on the dunes. Weston-super-Mare, because distantly retreating tides ensured from the beginning an emphasis on sand amusements and refreshments, sums up the pleasures of beach meals for the seaside in general, with its series of old timber huts on the beach, each with the same simple wooden forms and tables at which our grandparents ate as children. There, generation upon generation has bought lemonade and tea, sweets and chocolates, as well as buckets and spades or solid chunks of nourishing cake to top up beach picnic baskets, perhaps consumed to the strains of a song like:

> One, two three
> My mother caught a flea,
> Put it in the teapot
> And made a cup of tea

or a version of the National Anthem never sung within a real Majesty's hearing:

> Happy and glorious,
> Three slices for four of us,
> Thank the Lord there's no more of us!
> God Save the Queen.

Proprietors of tea gardens everywhere have long fancied themselves as poets who, though rarely in Wordsworth's league, nevertheless show splendid turns of humour in making the points that refreshments are available and that their wrappings are not intended as additional paving material on the path. Here rhymes one of that breed beside the path to Anstey's Cove near Torquay, in both English and Latin tongues:

> Picnics supplied with Hot Water and Tea,
> At a nice little house down by the Sea;
> Fresh Crabs and Lobsters every day,
> Salmon peel; sometimes Red Mullet and Grey;
> The neatest of pleasure boats let out on hire,
> Fishing Tackle as good as you can Desire;
> Bathing Machines for Ladies are kept,
> With Towels and Gowns, all quite Correct;
> THOMAS is the Man who supplies Everything,
> And also teaches Young People to Swim.

Anstey's Cove, with so much added to charming surroundings, was perfect whether Mother's hamper contained the bread-and-scrape (margarine very thinly spread) of families barely able to afford one visit in five years or the bun fight (many and varied goodies) of better-placed parents. Both tasted equally good.

Crumbs fed to the birds, flasks emptied and tummies replete, the time came round for a final visit to the nearest kiosk, for sticks of local rock, each with the resort's name in pink lettering, running right through the middle.

How did the words Torquay or Blackpool get there? Sophisticated 1951 was as mystified as 1901 on this great seaside question, sufficiently to justify a special display in the seaside section of the Festival of Britain exhibition.

Blackpool, queen of rock-selling resorts should perhaps claim also rock's origin, but honesty bids local history to share the credit with Morecambe and with inland Dewsbury.

At Dewsbury, a mining community far removed from any beach atmosphere, a miner is said to have hung up his coal grimed boots for the last time one day in 1868 to devote his time to toffee-making. Two years later the miner's shop was offering a more original sweetmeat: long sticks of brittle rock, with the title of a popular song, 'WHOA! EMMA!', inscribed inside throughout its length.

Dewsbury, Morecambe and Blackpool all today claim rock's origin, but Blackpool remains the acknowledged centre of the trade, rivalled only by Merry Margate. How the lettering gets inside is still the pleasantest mystery of the seaside until a child is taken to see for

Feeding her face, as the saying went; hats were always worn in summer in the 1930s.

'Cockles! Whelks! Mussels!': a Welsh cockle woman of about 1926.

Picnicking in high summer one year in the late 1920s, swathed in furs and felt hats.

himself how glucose and suger are boiled to about 300°F into a bubbling thick mass of flavoured goo, then poured onto a warm surface for working, and how coloured portions are removed for use in lettering while the rest, going white, is worked into the outer layers. The secret of rock lettering lies in the original size of each strip and the white strips around which it is rolled, initially the shape and size of a rolled carpet, large enought for moulding into such difficult characters as 'B' (the entire word Blackpool reputedly requires only seven minutes work), which afterwards are packed down smaller and smaller until the word is only about an inch long. Some are comparatively simple; the letter 'O' is merely a strip of white rock with a red coating, condensed down to size. Six or seven rock-making concerns still flourish in Blackpool, producing two tons of rock a day in summer; in winter the trade continues, supplying such diverse tourist spots as Niagara Falls and Spain.

Ginger ale and ginger beer were always statutory requirements for picnicking, acceptable to everyone from Uncle Bill, currently 'on the wagon' after signing the Pledge, to pale Aunt Fanny, in an age when teetotalism was beginning to rival its parent, alcoholism, in universal popularity, though few who came to Blackpool and swigged self-righteously at lemonade and pop knew that this area was indeed the cradle of abstinence as well as of rock. England's earliest total abstinence society was formed in Lancashire in 1830 and became a nationwide movement largely through the issue of a new paper, the Preston *Temperance Advocate*. Three years later Richard Turner, a working-class orator of burning convictions against alcohol, found himself frustratingly stuck for the right word to arouse a lukewarm Preston audience, to embody the quintessence of his beliefs. His message was not mere abstinence from spirits but absolute abandonment of all strong liquor, to which labourers habitually turned with some justification rather then drink water known to be often riddled with cholera

112

Swanage picnic party with baby in splendid black perambulator.

germs. How to convey his complete conviction? Turner needed an expression implying something even more total than the word 'total', as if that term were written in fire and spelled with a 'T' of double strength. Inspiration dawned: T-Total, a double emphatic extension of simple 'total'. From one man's ardour a new dictionary word was coined, and the age of ginger beer for adults as well as children was born.

Ginger pop and ginger beer continued to be mainstays of picnicking until after the Second World War, when the Coca-Cola cult overtook it, but the old products are nevertheless still consumed at the sea, more than anywhere else. At least a century of mothers incited their young to 'wet yer whistle' on these harmless beverages.

A stroll between bathing and entertainment: Weymouth sands in about 1900.

9. 'Who's for the Chonkabonk?'

Whether brought to Weymouth by horse-drawn carriage, to teeming Victorian Brighton by train or to Merry Margate of the 1930s by motorcoach, holiday-makers, once booked into lodgings, remained remarkably consistent in their leisure requirements. From the Third to the Sixth George, prime diversions would be sporting, tourism, bathing, reading, writing to Aunt Fanny at home and theatrical or musical entertainment. Between about 1810 and 1939 these changed their guise with changing times and fashions and with the emancipation of women but not their basic natures.

Sporting blood never ran redder than in the veins of Regency bucks, but only in the veins of men; women would not wield more than a delicate mallet or ride astride for another one and a half centuries. Sport ran from racecourse conventionality to such pastimes as shooting game composed of brick as well as feathers, led by a larking Prince whose notion of amusement was 'attempting to shoot doves with single balls', being 'esteemed a most excellent shot'; so accurate was Prinny that he allegedly also 'lowered the tops of several of the chimneys on the Hon. Mr Mindham's house' in the spirit of a modern gun knocking off clay pigeons.

Periodically fashionable Brighton removed itself from formal promenades to the high Downs, Brighton being noted for 'a fine racecourse with a stand capable of containing a considerable number of spectators'. Being seen there and acknowledged with a nod from the right people stamped a racegoer as gentry or pretending gentry, particularly in July and August when these races were 'well attended by persons of the highest distinction'.

Theatrical and musical entertainment whiled away many leisured evenings for Prinny's rich but sometimes raffish followers. 'The audience part is very handsome,' it was observed of Brighton's new Theatre Royal, 'furnished with two tiers of boxes and a large gallery, the whole . . . elegantly fitted up, particularly the box appropriated to the Prince'. Every aspiring rival resort built itself a theatre, including tiny East Bourne, unrecognisable from modern Eastbourne, where 'a small theatre and, at the Lamb Inn . . . a subscription ballroom, and a circulating library, may be reckoned among the amusements of the place.'

Gambling drew fashionable menfolk into evening huddles, as at 'Raggett's subscription house at the corner of the North Parade

Fashion (hired) becomes positively daring; note off-the-shoulder male costume.

[Brighton], which affords the votaries of gaming every facility for indulging their favourite propensity.'

To Brighton migrated London's best musicians at the Prince's behest, including the Irish singer Michael Kelly, whose Mozart interpretations were derived from the master himself, and the glittering young Rossini, operatic sensation of Italy. More Italian airs sounded from the outdoor bandstand in inartistic selections from the latest operas, equivalent to hit musicals of today, as crowds gathered at the Steyne, 'a favourite promenade of the fashionable visitors . . . every evening during the Season, when a small but select band performs for their amusement in a neat orchestra'.

Equestrianism as entertainment consistently drew crowds to the new Royal Circus of 1808, built 'chiefly for the exhibition of horsemanship'.

Touring, naturally, depended upon four-legged horsepower, as Society followed the Georges from Weymouth to fashionable minor spas or from Brighton over the South Downs, but river and sea journeys were also becoming popular for pleasure as well as purposeful conveyance; thus we read of 'vessels fitted up for the accommodation of passengers, like the Gravesend boats at London, sailing every tide from Ipswich to Harwich and back again, an excursion that is rendered truly delightful by the beauty of the surrounding scenery'.

'One theatre, a tolerably spacious edifice . . . two respectable libraries and commodious warm baths' made Georgian Worthing typical of better-patronised resorts; it also typified a preoccupation with lending and circulating libraries that was destined to endure through to the 1950s, mostly attached to booksellers' and stationers' emporia, lending out treacly light romances, wherein impossibly pure heroines were wooed by improbably handsome but unsuitable swains, to pale daughters and wives of visiting sportsmen.

115

"HURRAY, UNCLE! COME ALONG! HERE'S ANOTHER CIRCUS!"

Punch's view of
unintentional entertainment,
1908.

Guidebooks were dutifully bought or borrowed, lest some chink in
one's educational armour were exposed during dinnertable conversation. Wallowing in words, their authors plunged into fat, verbose
accounts whose titles alone were in effect paragraphs: *A Short History
of Brighthelmstone with Remarks on its Air and an Analysis of its
Waters, particularly an Uncommon Mineral one long Discovered
though but lately Used*; or *The Origin and Description of Bognor, or
Hothampton, and an Account of some Adjacent Villages*; or, again,
*The Imperial Guide to the Picturesque Scenery, Subjects of Antiquity
and Fashionable Resorts throughout the Coast of Suffolk to Yarmouth*,
to cite but three at random.

Victorian holiday-makers divided themselves into similar categories;
sporting, touring, literary and theatrical, the latter subdivided sharply
into professional and amateur, this being the heyday of drawing-room
theatricals and sing-songs, concert parties and amateur pianism.

Concert parties, pierrots and dance troupes drawn from one large
family were common, at amateur as well as professional level. Never
indeed was amateur entertainment more universal than in the pre-TV
days of the parlour piano; days when, after tea, Uncle John puffed out
his chest in *Pale Hands I Loved* or Gilbert and Sullivan's latest hit,
Auntie Min got out her recitations and Aunt Lottie performed the

116

shallow showy pieces of Sydney Smith and his fellows, all scales, arpeggios and 'twiddly bits', to rows of envious gaping cousins; Liszt aroused no greater admiration in Bath audiences than Auntie playing to the home gallery. Translated to a seaside boarding-house, Auntie happily played for guests' sing-songs (hymns of Sankey and Moody on Sundays), setting atremble the aspidistra drooping between framed pictures of the landlady's daughter's wedding. Sheet music sold in the town as readily as pop discs today, liberally advertised in the news-papers: 'New Song, *Light Of Heart*, Cavatina sung by Miss Birch, the poetry from *The Forgetmenot*, written by Charles Swain Esq., the music composed by John Barnett Price 2s', or, for those delighting in rummaging among piles of paper, 'Music at One-Third of the Price: Families and Amateurs are invited to Inspect extensive Collections in every Class of VOCAL and INSTRUMENTAL MUSIC by most favourite British and Foreign Composers . . . at only 4d in the Shilling, at R . . .'s Music Warehouse.'

Parlour games were the rage, from the drawing-rooms of Bleak House at Broadstairs, where Dickens habitually enjoyed Charades or Animal-Vegetable-Mineral (today's Twenty Questions), to Jones's Boarding Establishment, where visitors whiled away evenings playing Person-and-Thing or The Minister's Cat (The Minister's cat is an Awful/Big/Cuddly/Daring Cat, never anything worse beginning with B or D).

Victorian theatre ranged from blood and thunder melodrama down to music hall as the century progressed, whilst outdoors Vauxhall and Ranelagh, though dead or dying themselves, inspired smaller pleasure gardens anywhere from Woolwich dockland to Broadstairs, where Dickens and his friends enjoyed open air concerts and dancing. 'We enjoy ourselves amazingly,' wrote Dickens of his favourite resort.

Dancing had countless devotees, though locations were as yet termed ballrooms, considerably more artificial and select than the dance halls to come, as at Torquay where 'there are fine shops to visit . . . and your assemblies or balls at stated periods during the Season, for which purpose the . . . Hotel possesses a ballroom of sufficient size having an orchestra at its upper end', namely, a small stage or dais. Thousands of musicians, from barely adequate to extremely good, found regular employment in hotel ballroom and theatre bands, more varied in instrumentation than the later dance-band; an army not destined to be disbanded until talkies came.

Edwardian times saw stirrings of womens' liberation and liberalisa-tion in general of such hallowed institutions as old-fashioned Sundays. Sabbath pleasuring lost something of its sinfulness. Cycling became *de rigeur* for ladies as skirts became shorter and less voluminous. 'Tennis, anybody?' echoed on the sporty air in female tones, and legs began to show. Ladies' hands took a tentative grip on clubs and fishing rods, even cricket bats.

117

Beach theatre in about 1910.

Circulating libraries multiplied like record shops today, as reading became wider and such subjects as divorce and adultery became acceptable, attached to everything from baths and pumprooms to 'rooms' and boarding-houses, as an early Weymouth example demonstrates:

Cummins' furnished apartments, delightfully situated on the Esplanade, [have] a reading room and library connected with them, to which admission is obtained by a moderate subscription, and where one finds everything one desires in the way of periodicals and modern works — no mean recommendation to a lodging at Weymouth.

Tiny though emergent Bournemouth was, innocent as yet of even a shop, it could none the less be boasted that its 'marine library . . . has recently been enlarged and greatly improved with many upper and lower rooms, fit for a superior class of visitors who desire to occupy a place in a good boarding house and a most delightful marine residence.'

Touring burst its bounds in a manner undreamed before, no longer limited to the range of horses; by train and steamer as well as carriage visitors explored every cranny within miles of their resorts. Given an exotic description, anywhere lured crowds, from Dorset's so-called volcanoes to the Kingdom of Heaven, from explosions to islands and foreign countries. They flocked to the sea from inland, as well as inland from the sea, writing into railway history such episodes as Brighton's first excursion train, when no fewer than forty-five carriages started behind four engines on Easter Bank Holiday of 1844, adding a fifth engine and six more carriages a few miles out and the same again at Croydon; altogether fifty-seven jam-packed carriages and six locomotives gasped into Brighton four and a half hours later. Brighton of the aristocrats and invalids would never be the same, henceforth London-super-Mare for multitudes.

Everyone took to the road, seeking neighbouring sites and sights, knowingly throwing off the latest quotations to show their literary and topographical knowledge, such as a Torquay area doggerel by the son of the author of the famous *Ingoldsby Legends:*

> It's certainly odd that this part of the coast,
> While neighbouring Dorset gleams white as a ghost,
> Should look like anchovy sauce spread upon toast.

Everyone took also to the water, paddling down Mersey to Rhyl, or down Thames to Clacton and Southend, despite the fact that Father Thames, overcrowded with cattle boats, steamers, factory wastes and the capital's sewage, flowed steadily towards the climax of the Great Stink which forced even Parliament to adjourn, so evil was the stench beneath its Westminster windows, *Punch*'s nose, too, twitched in serenading this great open sewer:

> Filthy river, filthy river!
> Foul from London to the Nore!
> What art thou but one vast gutter,
> One tremendous common shore?
>
> All beside thy sludgy waters,
> All beside thy reeking ooze,
> Christian folks inhale memphitis,
> Which thy bubbling bosom brews.

Christian folks, all the same, regarded this as the best route to their own seasides.

Anything and everything became good excuse for special steamers and special trains, from fifty or more miles away, as when in 1850 seven tons of gunpowder were inserted into Seaford cliffs for constructing a new breakwater; from London and nearer towns puffed the explosion specials, bringing gaping crowds to cheer as 200,000 tons of Seaford collapsed into the Channel.

'Praise the sea; on shore remain,' wrote one John Florio, but thousands more took to old ocean as well as old river, braving the choppy unstabilised Channel for the thrill of landing for a whole day in France of Belgium and trying out their stiff Anglicised *'parlez-vous?'*. Day trips overseas are nothing new. Less familiar to ourselves was the attitude of some people towards seasickness, anticipating measles parties in deliberately courting trouble to overcome some medical condition. 'To the bilious', wrote a Victorian doctor,

instead of taking constant medicines, I recommend embarking, when the day is fine, on board a sailing packet or a steamer and cross over to Calais or Boulogne in hopes of being made seasick. This operation empties the stomach more effectually than can be done by means of emetics, so justly esteemed in cases of obstructed or regurgitating bile. This plan may be adopted two or three times in the course of a

want to be a
y Dog come to
THSEA

Within the box you'll find I bring
Something well worth examining.

A type of postcard rarely seen today: ten or a dozen miniature views unrolled from the dog's crate; postage was one old ha'penny (barely a quarter of a new penny).

119

ON THE SANDS AT OSTEND.

Master Tom (knowledge of French—nil). "I say, do I call you Madam, or Madymoiselle?"
Mademoiselle. "When one does not know, one says Madame, n'est ce pas, Monsieur?"

Day trips overseas are nothing new; *Punch* went to Ostend as early as 1898.

two or three months' residence, if occasion requires. It should invariably be followed by equitation or airings in a carriage, extended some distance into the country.

By the time Victoria's son settled onto the throne, travellers were flaunting their sea legs instead of enjoying the miseries of seasickness as a nasty medicine. 'Let none consider himself a hardened salt until he has emerged scatheless from the ordeal of a rough passage to the Channel Islands,' a Weymouth guide author enthused; 'To those to whom seasickness is unknown, this is a magnificent excursion.'

Nearer home the Lyme Regis 'volcano' of 1908 attracted curious spectators, drawn by the lazily curling smoke plumes giving this and Weymouth Bay the nicknames, Naples of England. The strange cliff phenomenon dated from January of that year, when a great section of rock and earth slid downwards to new levels and began smouldering from within. Sulphurous smoke creeping from numerous cracks and fissures undeniably was volcano-like, as spontaneous combustion, begun by action of water, started in underlying firestone beds of bituminous shale and iron pyrites. Not until June did the volcano 'erupt', as the main hummocky mound split apart to reveal a burned-out interior described as like a brick kiln. Other landslips in this area duly attracted tourists, but none so hypnotically as the Lyme Volcano.

'A big break!': cigarette card cartoon from about 1918.

Devonshire holidaymakers' boast was even better than visiting the Bay of Naples in England: having sailed to the Kingdom of Heaven and back. Lundy, governed by the Reverend Heaven, acquired its title from the first submarine cable link between island and mainland, inaugurated by his voice declaiming in double meaning, 'The Kingdom of Heaven rejoiceth.' Ilfracombe boatmen joyously cashed in with placards advertising 'Day Excursions to the Kingdom of Heaven'. In a sense, they did not exaggerate; the Reverend Heaven's kingdom was a heaven of peace, wild seascapes and wheeling birds, far from the madding mainland crowd.

As early as about 1912 car ferries existed, few though were the motorcars on English roads, as is evident from a contemporary Isle of Wight advertisment, 'Motor cars transferred to the Island . . . without being slung'.

Char-a-bancs, colloquially charries, sharries or chonkabonks, lined up on every seafront soon after the nineteenth and twentieth centuries' turn: big, bulky open cars consisting of body, windscreen, seats and little else but wheels. An element of lingering public suspicion can be sensed in advertising, as at Falmouth in 1911: 'Tours daily . . . subject to sufficient passengers being available and circumstances permitting'.

Chonkabonks were for the multitude. For more 'refeened' sojourners of moderate to good means, a horse-drawn carriage, or at least a cab, was the only suitable conveyance. 'Knollsea has no fashionable drives, but many very pleasant go-as-you-please routes can be taken,' it was said of Hardy's Knollsea or Swanage. Weymouth continued allegiance to the horse by advertising that 'there are several good livery stables in the town near the railway station.'

Cabs could be hired in most resorts for pleasant drives. 'For a one-horse vehicle the authorised charge by time is 3/- for one hour and ninepence for every additional quarter of an hour or portion thereof;

Chonkabonks took the multitude touring; this one charged 7s 6d (37½p) for the trip to Widecombe from Torquay in about 1928.

by distance, 1/- per mile, and 6d for any part thereof after the first; half these rates for the return journey,' Rhyl characteristically advertised and would continue doing so for at least two further decades.

Railway fares as the First World War got underway were low and trains good, rattling between Brighton and London in an hour, not surpassed today, at '8s 6d return first class, 4s 2½d second, plus War Supplement'. Londoners could still shrug off war at Southend for 4s 4d return (roughly 22p), a resort that had 'considerably more than doubled its population' in the preceding decade.

Some other resorts, at the opposite extreme, admitted trains to their hearts reluctantly, knowing that they meant farewell to exclusiveness. Thus laments Lyme Regis after the opening of its railway in 1908.

Within recent years Lyme Regis has emerged from the somewhat shy retirement of the beautiful rural surroundings in which it had hidden itself, and had also been hidden by its devoted admirers, who were jealous of their 'find' and none too anxious to blazon its attractions abroad; but the railway first broke in upon its aloofness and helped to restore it to the position among holiday resorts that it held more than a century ago, while recently the motor coach has made it the popular objective of a pilgrimage.

Sporty clothes and a sporty outlook for women as well as men coloured the off-duty earlier 1900s. Holiday guides were packed with advertisements for bicycles for sale or hire, routes attractive to cyclists, suggestions for spins on a bicycle-made-for-two, and for saddles, each maker duly claiming to be the world's best: 'For comfort awheel ride only . . .'s Saddles, the Saddles that Satisfy — famous because faultless'. Bicycling in certain cases allowed poorer families just to scrape a brief holiday, when even train fares were too heavy; it was not unknown for a married couple to cycle tandem from London to Brighton despite the wife's customary annual condition and for the husband to return alone, leaving her in hospital as the victim of a boarding-house miscarriage. Penny-farthing cycles continued to be ridden on promenades and in country lanes alike, weaving in and out of lumbering charabancs, though by the 1920s they were rarities enough to attract every camera-clicker within range.

Sporty, Old Chap might have been many a resort's slogan as the twentieth century entered its second decade. Rhyl's advertisement for 1913 was characteristic of them all: 'Bathing, boating, fishing, croquet, bowls, tennis, golf, concert bands and theatrical performances, hippodrome entertainments (equestrian), cinematograph films, skating rink, water chute, miniature, scenic and figure-eight railways, coach and motor tours, steamboat excursions'.

A conveyance leaves the Post Office daily at 10.30 am and 2.15 pm, returning at 2.45 pm and again subsequently as arranged; this vehicle carries players and visitors to the links for 1/- single and 1/6 return. The groundsman lives at the thatched cottage near the ninth green, and from him tickets may be obtained on payment of 1/6 per day, 5/- per week, or 15/- per month.

122

Open touring car of about 1929, here hired by a lover and his lass.

There was always someone at home to write to; postcards ranged from near obscenity to such whimsical humour as this.

Everything's "Thumbs Up" here.

So ran Swanage's golfing attractions. Better still were such resorts as Prestatyn in North Wales (2/- a round, 2/6 on Sundays, equal to 10p and 12½p decimalised), whose residential golf clubhouse doubled as a hotel 'from Saturday dinner to Monday breakfast at 21/- including golf', enabling worshippers to live, breathe, wash, eat and sleep with golf, debating scores and handicaps with holy reverence in like-minded company from dawn to after dusk. Their custom was manna to any resort priding itself upon its golf facilities; of Newquay it was seriously written that 'it is no exaggeration to say that, next to the railway, no cause has contributed so much to the success of Newquay as a holiday resort as the establishment and good management of the golf club.'

Tennis boomed as the 1900s swung towards the First World War. Most clubs opened their doors to visitors, though at an average shilling a day they compared unfavourably with municipal and commercial courts at only one old tanner daily, where anything from a shilling to five bob purchased a full week's play. Season tickets averaged £1.00 or a guinea, 'nets and balls provided'.

Quieter moments still automatically meant a good read instead of today's television, from the ubiquitous lending and circulating libraries. How good a read depended upon how much one was prepared to disgorge; many libraries divided themselves into 1st and 2nd grade subscriptions, or A and B, the higher rate embracing all titles including the latest sensations, whereas 2 or B subscriptions often applied only to books over a year old. A glance at suggested titles for holiday perusal indicates the literary standards of books for the masses: *Mr Witt's Widow*; *An Old Fogey*; *Love Made Manifest*; *Broken Bonds*; *Stolen Souls*; *A Race with Ruin*.

Between reads there was always Aunt Fanny to write to, on a sepia view selected from a corner of the shop whilst more uninhibited buyers roared aloud at the more jauntily displayed racks of luxuriant comic bosoms and elephantine female backsides that sold in thousands. At least there was no hurry to buy and catch the post; town Post Offices

The "Jovials"

The 'Jovials', a troupe of pierrots, live up to their name.

not only opened as early as 7 in the morning and closed on average between 7 pm and 9 pm but also did service for two or three hours on Sunday mornings and Bank Holidays.

Entertainment from the boards became ever more popularised, ever less cerebral, as the halls and variety topped the bill of fare. Skill in manipulating rabbits, flags, balls, wires and human bodies counted for Everyman infinitely above Shakespeare, as turn followed turn, their programme numbers flashed in red lights from beside the proscenium arch, to rum-te-tum rhythms or spine-prickling crescendos of drums from the warmly-lighted pit. Juggler succeeded contortionist, wire-walkers and conjurers followed comedy cyclists and escapologists, between songs by shapely masculinised scraps of feminine fluff in white tie and topper. *My Old Man's A Dustman* and *Daisy, Daisy* were lustily taken up by the audience. These were unintellectual but wonderfully happy evenings, sending an Empire-ful of holidaymakers back to their lodgings chorusing well known refrains.

The very words Pier Pavilion conjure up visions of concert parties, differing from stage companies in using costume but little or no scenery; of pierrots and young dancers all crimped and curled, as well as of melodrama and concerts of light music or band performances. Two or three times daily crowds trooped onto the pier for musical relaxation, admission and pier toll included. In a few places they still follow remarkably closely the old days, as at Worthing where an excellent small light orchestra still plays daily and nightly for the inclusive price, at time of writing, of only 15p.

Llandudno here gives a typical sample of Pavilion life at about the time of the Great War.

Every morning during the Season . . . an orchestra of forty performers gives a free concert on the spacious pier head, where there is sitting accommodation for 2000 persons where a spacious shelter with movable sides has been erected for use in wet weather . . . . During the afternoons and evenings performances are given by pierrots . . . . At the Pier Theatre of Varieties cinematograph exhibitions and variety entertainments are given.

Future plans rang ambitiously: 'A scheme has been put forward to erect a pier and pavilion in the centre of the bay . . . 1305 ft long by 40 ft wide . . . . The pierhead should be enclosed by glass screens, and shall have an area of 200 ft by 180 ft.'

Classical oratorio singers and stunt men overlapped with variety in popular esteem. Names from Queen's Hall as well as music hall were household words, as in that forerunner of pop-songs, *The World Turned Upside Down:*

> Sims Reeves was dancing a hornpipe,
> And Santley was doing a fling,
> And Blondin came down from the tightrope
> A tenor song to sing . . .
> As the world turned upside down.

Young variety-show dancer of about 1910.

Parlour games were universal and hilarious, among big family parties or drawing-rooms full of boarding-house guests. Person-and-Thing ran riotously, so did Charades, or a game requiring one person to leave the room and return to perform some small idiotic act agreed by the rest ('bite an inch off the poker', namely an inch away from it, or kiss the curate), everyone singing louder or softer according to whether the stooge's actions were 'hot', 'getting warmer' or 'cold', or far from the trail, to the ditty:

> Do you know the muffin man?
> Do you know the muffin man?
> Do you know the muffin man?
> That lives down Drury Lane?

With another George, George V, dawned the strenuous 1920s of flappers, flat chests, bar shoes, dropped waists, exposed knees, the Charleston and dance music with a kick in it. Elaborate mechanical organs as well as bands presided over our dance halls, ornately garlanded with flowers, fruit and cherubs, working on the old musical box principle but playing entire waltzes and marches from concertina-like folded books punched with holes, anticipating modern commercial tapes. Their tone was remarkably rich, whether produced by steam or, later, electricity.

The flicks truly flickered as silent baddies pursued handsome goodies for a lady's hand, to roulades of hurry-music, flight-music, country-music and town-music, changing to shameless melodic goo as lips met on the silver screen and the pianist launched into some popular love song. Two good stalls cost about 6d each (9d for the best), leaving funds for a shared bag of coconut ice out of an evening's tight budget.

Musical comedy graced the stage, more romantic and sentimental than modern musicals, always ending with the hero and heroine soaring to top As of ecstasy at curtain fall. Great shows lit the theatrical firmament of the 1920s and early 1930s: *Rose Marie*, *Chu Chin Chow*, *The Vagabond King*, *The Student Prince*, and many more. Ivor Novello stopped as many feminine hearts on stage as Valentino on screen. Beauties of theatre and cinema smiled through tiny pursed lips from glossy postcards in every gift shop. Operatic prima donnas, too, had such followings that the demise of a top name inspired special window displays throughout the land, around large black draped photographs, provided she had sung her way into the public's heart with *Home Sweet Home* or *I Dream't That I Dwelt In Marble Halls*. Selections of melodies from musical comedies and operettas formed the backbone of light music, a craze of doubtful value when extended to less oom-pah-pah operas than *Il Trovatore*. Names went up in new-fangled neon instead of flares, a garish fancy for which conservative grandmas could find no good word; 'Those *horrible* lights, dear,' was a terrible epithet from one who never swore worse than 'bother'.

126

In the sketch: *Edith Day. in Rose Marie.* 9.9.26.

Original pencil sketch made in 1926 of Edith Day in *Rose Marie*.

Most larger hotels continued to maintain their own resident bands or orchestras, versatile ensembles capable of reading any new hit at sight or new dances, preserving smart rhythm from cocktail time to after midnight without benefit of microphones or singers untrained in singing. Countless brother instrumentalists found regular employment in municipal seaside groups, from a handful on a pier to Bournemouth's full-sized orchestra. 'It is believed that Eastbourne supplies more free music of a high class character than any other seaside town,' it was claimed in about 1921; what would Torquay, Worthing or Bournemouth have replied?

THE "CORRICK FAMILY" ENTERTAINERS.

Typical family troupe of entertainers, 'open for engagements'.

For sheer variety of entertainments and amusements in one complex, Dreamland at Margate was hard to rival, the former Hall By The Sea boasting not only its famous and still extant funfair but also acres of gardens with intricate fountains, a fine ballroom, concert halls, cafes, a monster scenic railway (big dipper in modern speech), and a super-cinema, the word super indicating two thousand or more seats facing a giant screen. Most larger resorts built similar centres, notably the Southend Kursaal and those at Clacton and Blackpool. Some incorporated existing landmarks; what is today's Littlehampton helter-skelter but a former windmill?

Conceptions of the sacrosanct altered radically as golf courses opened on Sundays and even Good Friday, to women as well as men. 'Good Friday to the following Wednesday inclusive, five shillings per day' advertised Newquay, luring further patrons with the bait of a 20 per cent reduction for families of three of more. Fees usually differentiated between ladies and gentlemen. Ladies paid 2/- a day, 7/6 a week at Bude while men perforce forked out 5/- and 15/-, though another local course struck a fairer blow for equality with 'Ladies using the Long Course pay the same fees as gentlemen.'

Calmer pursuits still catered for those who believed that women should be frilly, feminine and fragile and should not stride around in semi-masculine garb. Eastbourne's croquet club welcomed visitors known to members at ten shillings a week, but plenty of purely male preserves none the less remained sacred, notably the billiards and snooker halls found above the shops in most resort high streets.

Chonkabonks had come to stay, a popular choice both for driving on arrival and for making the outward journey. 'Coaching by car is more successful than ever before,' concluded one newspaper of 1923 as coach after coach left London for Torquay, Bournemouth and elsewhere at nine guineas all-in for Easter. Fares had actually fallen compared with the previous season, so fierce was competition for custom, and a further 10 per cent reduction was promised for summer. Gadgetry and gimmickry worked overtime, clambering onto the bandwagon of profit with such devices as the Silent Guide Scenaidicator: 'No need to be ignorant. No need to ask. The Silent Guide tells you *silently* of the places through which you pass. You will find it installed on the best Motor Coaches in most Holiday Resorts.'

Private motoring was on the upturn. Lovers and honeymooners daringly hired open tourers for driving wives and fiancées into the country from their holiday diggings, to sputters of exhaust and clatters of hard wheels. 'Special Feature: GARAGE attached to Hotel accommodating 25 cars, petrol and oil pumps installed' became as common a landlord's lure as 'Electric light in ALL rooms'. Corporations advertised 'Parking spaces for private motor cars', taking all of six to a dozen; as many as twenty spaces could be found in a large town such as Eastbourne, for that rakish, raffish modernist minority who preferred horsepower fed on petrol instead of hay.

Motorised and horse-drawn days thus overlapped, up to the brink of another world war, as is clear in the Newquay of 1922: 'A variety of conveyances may be hired, from little pony traps or ''jingles'' to motors and four-horse brakes,' the latter having long benches sideways on instead of double seats facing front.

Holiday-making mankind ventured also into the air, sustained by such standbys as 'M . . .'s Seasick Remedy (''Stops and prevents travel sickness . . . and all stomach disorders caused by the motions of sea, train, auto, car or air travel'')'.

Trains continued to operate mainly under steam into the 1930s, except in the electrified London suburbs and on the short Brighton line, as some of history's most majestic steam locomotives, including the celebrated world speed record breaker, *Mallard*, puffed across the land. Many a holiday was partially spoiled by Mother getting an obstinate smut in her eye through an open window; but many a holiday was made by the childish thrill of running to the front on arrival to say Thank You for a safe journey to the driver and fireman, grinning sooty demons made ruddy faced by the blazing glow from the open firebox door and smelling of coal and hot oil. Long distance trains would never be trains again once diesel displaced steam and named trains went out of favour: The Cornish Riviera Express, Bournemouth Belle and Brighton Belle had an aura that was more even than dark-panelled Pullman cars and red-shaded lights, one that today's preserved steam lines cannot quite recapture.

Sport continued as a holiday preoccupation, backed by the more expensive hotels as a trade push. 'Golf trophy for competition at any time during each three months — best bogey score under handicap — on any local course,' appeared in Eastbourne literature, whilst Margate staged special Sunday afternoon cricket tournaments between leading hotels' guests.

The day of the elegant *thé dansant* was at its height. Better-heeled visitors danced in the late afternoon in Pavilions and Winter Gardens to small select bands, between thin sandwiches and pricey decorated cakes taken at small bamboo tables, waited upon by bobbed waitresses in frilled white aprons, half-smothered in potted palms.

They were high, heady, balmy and barmy days, those passing 1930s. Make hay while the sun shines, make sandcastles while the beach is free and open, might have been their mottoes. It was almost as if their self indulgent preoccupation with amusements, dancing and pleasures had a fatalistic undercurrent; as though instinct sensed that the end of the 1930s would be more than the mere end of a calendar era, after which the seaside would never be quite as it had been for the past hundred happy years.

Dreamland, Mecca of all Margate entertainment-seekers, rears up in the background of this 1930s beach scene.

10. *Never Quite the Same*

Burning crimson sank the sun, that certain summer evening in 1939, a huge seething ball low on a thundery, threatening horizon, so red it might have been composed from blood of the slain of an entire war.

Something indefinably sinister about the great natural blood-orange temporarily overawed even a child, who had gambolled all day on Herne Bay beach, unaware that the end of her little seaside world was at hand. 'It seems almost like an omen, dears,' remarked Granny, staring from the homegoing train as the sun vanished behind lashing sheets of torrential rain. Moaning winds tore through Kentish orchards. Trees, bending towards the earth, were continually floodlit by lightning, glimpsed through clouds of white steam blown downwards from the engine, to cling damply on sodden windowpanes. No ordinary sunset and storm were these. Granny, whose words so often held almost Biblical wisdom, was right yet again. They *were* omens.

Within a month England had plunged into war. Beaches became deserted. Barbed-wire entanglements and tank traps replaced rows of deckchairs and sweet kiosks. Gaping holes appeared in piers where planks were removed half way along to discourage their use by invaders, particularly in Kent, or Hell Fire Corner. In the west, some resorts stayed in modified business, like Weston-super-Mare and Burnham-on-Sea, gamely catering for localised Sunday School outings or bombed-out Bristolians seeking brief forgetfulness.

In 1945 came austere peace, and by next season seaside life appeared to be returning to normal, attracting crowds so starved of relaxation that a pier with a gap in its middle was a small inconvenience. *Eagle* steamers, returned from life-saving at Dunkirk, once more plied from Tower Pier to Southend and Margate, 'black with people'. Bands struck up afresh on refurbished promenades; one resort, Bournemouth, went further, expanding Dan Godfrey's musical ensemble, depleted during wartime, into a unique seaside-based symphony orchestra, under the newly-arrived young Rudolf Schwarz. Pavilion shows opened again, against makeshift scenery and costumes (clothing and other ration coupons still applied). Life on its surface was apparently the same, or even better.

Only apparently, and only on the surface. Before the 1950s were half over, truth prevailed. Things were *not* the same. Family cars, formerly luxuries, became swiftly universal, destroying steamers'

Latter-day paddle steamer in the Bristol Channel.

monopoly. Television created new standards of theatrical entertainment, having appeared on the 'telly' becoming accepted proof of a performer's ability; the name was the draw, not the show. European holidays became ever cheaper and more enticing, within the pockets of office girls. Cruising costs fell to moderate Civil Servant level. So many rival attractions arose to tempt a new, more *blasé* generation away from unsophisticated pleasures which were good enough for their dads. Compared with the Costa Brava, Brighton or Bridlington were Old Hat, fit only for elderly aunts, not well-paid bricklayers. Longer and longer paid annual holidays destroyed the thrill of Bank Holidays.

Steamer sailings became reduced to holiday sidelights instead of high-lights, between runs in one's own compact black box of a car, in which the family also made the outward and return journeys, lessening still more the transport monopoly of steamships and steam trains. Another decade, and the *Eagles* were gone, with the *Bristol* and *Cardiff Queens*, the famous paddler *Princess Elizabeth*, and numberless fine ships with years of useful life in them, suddenly consigned to breakers' yards or laid-up.

Their passing, possibly more than any other factor, symbolised the fact that 150 years of England's seaside-going were gone. The future held no more place for their easy-going pace, compared with roaring powerboats, than post-war seasiders had further use for one-piece suits instead of bikinis or for hutch-like huts instead of stripping on the beach.

132

The Second World War thus acted as a full-stop in the narrative of seaside life and pleasures. Succeeding paragraphs — the following three decades — would tell very different stories.

Going down to the sea in ships or puffing trains was destined never to be the same as in the period of bathing-machines, or as when gasps of amazement greeted the first baggy pairs of bloomers strolling along the Prom-prom- prom-tiddly-om-pom-pom.

Yesterday, today, tomorrow; the seaside will never again be as it was before the Second World War, yet childhood and the sea themselves will always be the same.

Bibliography

Clunn, H. P.   *Face of the Home Counties*
Defoe, D.   *Tour Through the Whole Island of Great Britain*, 1724
Granville, A. B.   *Spas of England and Principal Sea-Bathing Places*, 1840
Jerrold, W.   *Highways & Byways in Kent*, 1923
Lucas, E. V.   *Highways & Byways in Sussex*, 1904
Thorne, J.   *Handbook to the Environs of London*, 1875
Mayhew, H.   *London Life and the London Poor*, 1851
Payne, D.   *Dorset Harbours*, 1953
Rogers, H. C. B. *Turnpike to Iron Road*, 1961
Shoberl, F.   *The Beauties of England & Wales; Suffolk and Sussex*, 1815
Ward Lock Red Guide series, 1907 to 1927

Acknowledgments

The author wishes sincerely to thank those who help has made this volume possible and in particular the following: Miss Irene Searle, for loan of the pictures on pages 15, 21, 22, 24(2), 29, 31, 37, 40, 41, 54, 68, 69, 70, 71, 75, 76, 79, 80, 83, 85, 89 (bottom), 99, 101, 103, 113 (top), 115, 123 (bottom), 124, 125, 128; Mrs E. R. (Nellie) Searle, her mother, for those on pages 35, 39, 40, 49, 57, 104(2), 111 (top), 112, 121, 123 (top), 127 and 130, and for a great deal of background material; Mr A.C.N. (Noel) Searle, her father, for the pictures on pages 32 and 33; The Gladys Wright Collection for loan of the historic postcards reproduced on pages 7, 18, 22 (top), 51, 59, 60, 66 and 98; Ward Lock Ltd., for permission to quote from the Red Guides to Weymouth (1907), Llandudno (1913), Eastbourne (1927), Bude (1921) and Lyme Regis (1927) and also The Salvation Army, the Church Army and Shaftesbury Society, and Blackpool Reference Library. The illustration on page 8 is reproduced by permission of Brighton Borough Council. The cartoons on pages 9, 12, 44, 56, 63, 77, 82, 84, 86(2), 100, 107 and 116 appear by permission of *Punch*. The pictures on pages 4, 19, 23, 26-7, 30, 45, 46, 47, 50, 58, 64, 72, 102, 108, 109, 113 (bottom) and 118 are from the Mansell Collection; those on pages 81, 89 (top), 132 and 133 come from the author's collection. End paper illustration by permission of Brighton Borough Council.

Index